CALVARY REVISITED

Lenten Sermons

Erich Heintzen

and

O. P. Kretzmann

Publishing House
St. Louis   London

Concordia Publishing House, St. Louis, Missouri
Concordia Publishing House Ltd., London, E. C. 1
Copyright © 1973 Concordia Publishing House
Library of Congress Catalog Card No. 73-10909
ISBN 0-570-03178-8

MANUFACTURED IN THE UNITED STATES OF AMERICA

CONTENTS

WERE YOU THERE —

WERE YOU THERE

When He Was Betrayed?

While He was still speaking, Judas came, one of the twelve, and with him a great crowd with swords and clubs, from the chief priests and the elders of the people. Now the betrayer had given them a sign, saying, "The one I shall kiss is the man; seize him." And he came up to Jesus at once and said, "Hail, Master!" And he kissed Him. Jesus said to him, "Friend, why are you here?" Then they came up and laid hands on Jesus and seized Him. And behold, one of those who were with Jesus stretched out his hand and drew his sword, and struck the slave of the high priest, and cut off his ear. Then Jesus said to him, "Put your sword back into its place; for all who take the sword will perish by the sword. Do you think that I cannot appeal to My Father, and He will at once send Me more than twelve legions of angels? But how then should the Scriptures be fulfilled, that it must be so?" At that hour Jesus said to the crowds, "Have you come out as against a robber, with swords and clubs to capture Me? Day after day I sat in the temple teaching, and you did not seize Me. But all this has taken place that the Scriptures of the prophets might be fulfilled." Then all the disciples forsook Him and fled.

MATTHEW 26:47-56, ESPECIALLY VV. 48-49

7

We who live in this age of the jet plane, television, and deep-freeze — what possible connection can we have with something that happened 2,000 years ago in the days of chariots, togas, and torchlights? Our relation to the distant past may on the surface seem hazy and remote. Actually, we are more closely bound up with the past than we sometimes think. This is true in a unique way of our relation to the suffering and death of our Lord Jesus Christ. The very fact that we commonly say "our" Lord Jesus is evidence that we know and feel this connection.

During these special midweek Lenten services, let us try to bring our connection with the suffering and death of our Lord into sharper focus. Let us endeavor to recapture for ourselves, and to make plain to others, the relevance of the Passion to our time, using the searching theme, "Were You There?" This evening we ask:

WERE YOU THERE WHEN HE WAS BETRAYED?

I

Let us see who was there.

Judas was there. Judas, the man from Kerioth, was one of the twelve men chosen by Jesus to be His disciples. Jesus loved him as much as He loved the others; in fact, Judas held a special office in the group: he was the treasurer. But the Scripture also tells us Judas was a thief. Greed, covetousness, finally drove him to betray his Lord to His enemies for 30 pieces of silver — not a large sum. The text briefly describes the actual betrayal in the Garden of Gethsemane: "While He was still speaking, Judas came, one of the twelve, and with him a great crowd with swords and clubs, from the chief priests and the elders of the people. Now the betrayer had given them a sign, saying, 'The one I shall kiss is the man; seize him.' And he came up to Jesus at once and said, 'Hail, Master!' And he kissed Him. Jesus said to him, 'Friend, why are you here?' Then they came up and laid hands on Jesus and seized Him." (Vv. 47-50)

The question how Judas, who had lived and walked and talked with the Savior, could do such a thing is perhaps not so very difficult to answer. He had a special weakness and gave in to it from time to time. Finally, we read, Satan entered into his heart and maneuvered him into striking the fatal bargain. Bitter remorse later on did not help Judas, but drove him to hopeless despair and self-murder—"he went and hanged himself." Judas did not realize that when he first gave in to temptation and ignored Christ, he thereby placed the noose around his neck. Later events only helped to tighten the noose. It is an old, old story with men.

Look into the shadows of Gethsemane again. You will see that the chief priests and elders of the people were there. These were the people who gladly paid Judas to betray Jesus to them in the garden. Why did they hate Jesus so? Why did they want Him out of the way? Again, the answer is not difficult. They were jealous of Him. They resented and feared His rising popularity with the people. "Look, the world has gone after Him," they cried frantically (John 12:19). Resentment, envy, jealousy so overwhelmed their hearts that they plotted the death of Jesus and looked for someone to "put the finger" on Him. There is added shame here because these were the religious leaders, churchmen, who claimed to be God's spokesmen.

The chief priests and elders and Judas were the chief conspirators in the betrayal. But others were indirectly involved. There was the mob of temple police, henchmen and hangers-on, who came with swords and clubs or brickbats. For the most part, they did not know what it was all about. They probably did not care. They were blindly following their leaders. They unthinkingly helped add to the suffering of the innocent Christ.

The disciples were there. Although they had nothing directly to do with betraying Jesus, they did not help Him either. Simon Peter drew his sword to defend his Lord by force. On behalf of Jesus, Peter cut off the right ear of the servant of the high priest. This was misguided, fanatical zeal at its worst. Jesus rebuked His disciple and healed His enemy. Then Peter and the other disciples, filled with bewilderment and fear, forsook Him and fled.

II

Now, let's for a moment forget *who* was there and consider *what* was there — what was in the hearts and minds of these people, what were their attitudes and motives. And what we find there is not so very strange to us today.

There was greed and covetousness that betrayed Jesus. We may call it materialism, that is, an undue regard for money and material things. It is the spirit that puts things before principles, that puts success and the physical comforts of life before the love of God and His holy will. When a twentieth-century disciple of Jesus Christ gives up something of Christ in his business, social, or school life to get something from the world, he is betraying Christ for a price. Can you say that you have never at any time in your life come to terms with the world at Christ's expense? No? Then you were there in the garden.

What else was there? There was envy and jealousy that betrayed Christ. Have you been envious or jealous of anyone in such a way that you begrudged the other person what he had? Disliked and perhaps even secretly hated that person? If so, then you were there in the garden. Whatever hurts one of God's children hurts Him too.

There was blind following of worldly-minded leaders that helped betray Jesus. Many in the mob were just "following the crowd." Have you ever thoughtlessly "followed the crowd" in something that you later felt was an insult and offense to Christ? If so, then you were there in the garden. Remember, before following the crowd, know where the crowd is going.

There was also misguided zeal and fear-inspired faithlessness at the betrayal of Jesus. Think! Have you ever attempted to defend Christ, if not by physical violence, then by force of the sharp word, or by a loveless attack upon His enemies? Or have you ever for fear of ridicule "clammed up" so that it amounted to forsaking Him and fleeing? If so, then you were in the garden with Him that night. In St. Mark's account of the betrayal special mention is made of a certain young man that followed Jesus. When the arresting party tried to seize him, he fled, leaving his clothes clutched in their hands. The young man is not identified, his name is a blank. Why, I don't know. But I wonder whether God has not left it blank so that each of us might see himself in that young man and write his own name there.

Yes, in some way or other we disciples of today can see ourselves in the behavior of all those who were with Him in the garden in the night in which He was betrayed. We cannot feel smug as we read the history of the Passion of our Lord. You were there. I was there. And if we were there, we too are responsible for what went on there. This is what the writer of the hymn says when he writes:

> My burden in Thy Passion,
> Lord, Thou hast borne for me,

For it was my transgression
Which brought this woe on Thee.

III

And this brings us to Him who was betrayed in the garden, Jesus, the Lamb of God, who takes away the sin of the world.

And in Him, too, we see ourselves intimately related to what took place in the garden and in the judgment hall and on Calvary. We are, then, not only connected with the betrayers but also with Him who was betrayed. This is what Isaiah means when he says: "Surely He has borne our griefs and carried our sorrows. . . . But He was wounded for our transgressions, He was bruised for our iniquities; upon Him was the chastisement that made us whole, and with His stripes we are healed. All we like sheep have gone astray; we have turned every one to his own way; and the Lord has laid on Him the iniquity of us all." (Is. 53:4-6)

In these words the prophet connects the whole human race with the suffering of Christ, because Christ is the sinner's Substitute. So we were "there" in the garden in the person of Christ, our Substitute. A substitute is one who takes another's place, does for another what that one is unable to do. By His perfect obedience to His Father's will He kept God's will for us. And more, with His innocent suffering and death He paid for the sins of those who made Him suffer. As He in the garden healed the ear of the servant of the high priest, His enemy, so has He cleansed us from our transgressions and restored us to life and true sonship with God our Father.

It is, then, in Him alone that we find the power today to overcome those sinful attitudes and motives that still beset the world. How often covetousness, jealousy, envy, misguided zeal, and fear still come between us and our God and between us and our fellowmen in home, in business, in politics, in school! But if He has atoned for our sin, He will also help us to overcome our weaknesses. "For we have not a high priest who is unable to sympathize with our weaknesses, but one who in every respect has been tempted as we are, yet without sin. Let us then with confidence draw near to the throne of grace, that we may receive mercy and find grace to help in time of need." (Heb. 4:15-16)

By His matchless mercy our sins against Him in the garden have been forgiven us. God for Jesus' sake remembers them no more. We are His own forever. We look with eager hope to see Him again in glory and to share His fellowship there. Take His precious promise to heart once again: "Where I am, there shall My servant be also." Amen.

WERE YOU THERE

When He Was Denied?

Then they seized Him and led Him away, bringing Him into the high priest's house. Peter followed at a distance; and when they had kindled a fire in the middle of the courtyard and sat down together, Peter sat among them. Then a maid, seeing him as he sat in the light and gazing at him, said, "This man also was with Him." But he denied it, saying, "Woman, I do not know Him." And a little later someone else saw him and said, "You also are one of them." But Peter said, "Man, I am not." And after an interval of about an hour still another insisted, saying, "Certainly this man also was with Him; for he is a Galilean." But Peter said, "Man, I do not know what you are saying." And immediately, while he was still speaking, the cock crowed. And the Lord turned and looked at Peter. And Peter remembered the word of the Lord, how He had said to him, "Before the cock crows today, you will deny Me three times." And he went out and wept bitterly.

LUKE 22:54-62

It is possible to view the tragic drama of Christ's suffering and death, from Gethsemane to Calvary, and be filled with nothing more than pity and sorrow for the bruised and bleeding Christ. That would be much the same as watching a sad play or movie, having a good cry, and then going unconcerned about our business. And that would be a tragedy.

It is our purpose during these midweek Lenten services to try to erase as much as possible the idea of actors and audience as we consider the Passion, and to see ourselves involved as participants in the divine drama. For what we see is really the acting out of the drama of the world's redemption, and that includes us all. We are essentially in the cast—not in the audience.

Therefore, we have chosen the theme "Were You There?" This evening we ask

WERE YOU THERE
WHEN HE WAS DENIED?

I

Let us see. After the flight of the disciples from the garden where they saw their Master betrayed, Peter was drawn back. He followed the mob and the bound Prisoner at a safe distance to the palace of the high priest. There was another disciple who returned after his first flight. That was John, who was for some reason known about the high priest's palace. It was John who got Peter into the courtyard of the palace. Then the two were apparently separated. It was chilly in the early morning hours, and Peter warmed himself by the fire in the hall. This was the setting for his threefold denial of his Lord. The text gives us the details of this memorable moment in simple, unadorned language: "Then a maid, seeing him as he sat in the light and gazing at him, said, 'This man also was with Him.' But he denied it, saying, 'Woman, I do not know Him.' And a little later someone else saw him and said, 'You also are one of them.' But Peter said, 'Man, I am

15

not.' And after an interval of about an hour still another insisted, saying, 'Certainly this man also was with Him; for he is a Galilean.' But Peter said, 'Man, I do not know what you are saying.' And immediately, while he was still speaking, the cock crowed." (Vv. 56-60)

Second to the tragedy of the betrayal by Judas in the garden is this denial by Peter in the palace of the high priest. In one way, it is even more shameful. The traitor, as far as we know, had never made any special claims of superior loyalty to the Master, but Peter certainly had. On several occasions he had vigorously proclaimed his undying allegiance to Jesus. Even in the face of the Master's warning, Peter avowed, "Though they all fall away because of You, I will never fall away" (Matt. 26:33). That was going out pretty far on the limb. But hear this same disciple again: "Lord, I am ready to go with You to prison and to death" (Luke 22:33). Later, after he was converted and strengthened by Jesus, he was ready. But not yet. In the high priest's palace, Peter was ready only to deny Jesus in order to save himself from prison and death.

Here we see Peter, the "rock" man. But he is a rock with chinks and cracks in it. Only in Christ was he truly a rock. Apart from Christ he is crumbling sandstone. Yet, while Peter was vehemently denying Him, He was willingly enduring the insults and the shame for the sake of truth and for the salvation of Peter and all like him.

II

As we look back over the scene of Peter's denial, we can clearly see the several stages of his great sin.

First, there were good intentions. But good intentions based on the flimsy foundations of human pride. Someone has said that "the road to hell is paved with good intentions." Good intentions are no better than the spirit which is behind them. And Peter's spirit was one of spiritual cocksureness. He thought himself so much better than others in his relation to Christ. Others might fail Christ; Peter, never!

When you heard of a neighbor or fellow Christian who in a moment of weakness fell headlong into sin, did you ever ask, "How could he ever do a thing like that?" Was there perhaps behind that question this thought, "I'd never do a thing like that"? Watch it! That's the same spirit that tripped up Peter.

Another step in Peter's denial was his stubborn refusal to listen to the warnings of Jesus. Jesus similarly warns us through His Word: "Let anyone who thinks that he stands take heed lest he fall" (1 Cor. 10:12). Again, "Watch and pray that you may not enter into temptation" (Mark 14:38). Yet, how often we fail to listen. We don't say it, but we think something like this: "Yes, I heard you Lord. But I know what I'm doing. I can take care of myself." Do you know, that's just what Peter thought!

Then there was Peter's association with the wrong people. Whatever it was that brought him back, it was not to help Jesus. When he was recognized, Peter became panic stricken. In order to save himself, he tried to dissociate himself from Jesus and to identify himself with His enemies. He began to curse and to swear. It was as much as to say, "Look, boys, I'm one of you." Many others who merely meant to warm themselves at the enemy's fire have gotten themselves badly burned.

But not all denials of our Lord are as direct as Peter's was. Silence may also be eloquent. The other disciples in a way were in this too. They hid and were silent. Today, too, Christ is denied and pained by too many silent Christians in the world. Are some of us among them?

Finally, we can see the progressiveness of sin, climaxed by the shameful rejection of Christ by one who promised to go with Him into prison and to death. When you take the first step, although a small step, in dissociating yourself from Christ, you never know where it will end. Among people you know, possibly with whom you were confirmed, are some who are no longer among the disciples of the Lord. But their defection and ultimate denial was no doubt a gradual process. How is it with you? In which direction are you going? Toward Christ, or away from Him? Face this question honestly tonight.

If you can see yourself anywhere along the way in the stages of Peter's denial — and who of us can say he can't? — then you were there with Peter in those dark shadows of the high priest's palace. Let us make no mistake about it, it's no different just because the spirit of denial is found in us today. The sin of denying the Lord knows no one age or era. The sin that wounded Jesus and which He bore is inherent in the human heart the world over. "Sin came into the world through one man [Adam] and death through sin, and so death spread to all men because all men sinned" (Rom. 5:12). Yes, we — you and I — were there with Peter.

III

But the incident of the denial does not end so tragically as did that of the betrayal. After Peter's third disavowal we read: "And immediately, while he was still speaking, the cock crowed. And the Lord turned and looked at Peter. And Peter remembered the word of the Lord, how He had said to him, 'Before the cock crows today, you will deny Me three times.' And he went out and wept bitterly." (Vv. 60-62)

18

The love of Jesus did not abandon His faithless disciple, but searched him out. Perhaps it was while Jesus was being led from one part of the building to another that He caught Peter's eye. When Peter looked into the eyes of the Lord, he saw rebuke and hurt, but also pity and forgiveness. In the eyes of Jesus, Peter saw himself as he was, and he also saw once again who Jesus was. We know that the Lord not only forgave Peter but later also reinstated him into discipleship, drawing from him a threefold profession of love, though now spoken in the spirit of humble faith.

What you see here of Jesus' forgiving love is also for you. For you, too, share in the blessings of His Passion, forgiveness and pardon from all your sin—also the sin of denial. If you were there in Peter's denial, you are also included in Jesus' forgiveness. Have you received it, made it your own, by faith?

What shall we do in the light of His matchless love?

Let us from now on deny ourselves, not Him. This is true discipleship: "If any man would come after Me, let him deny himself and take up his cross and follow Me. For whoever would save his life will lose it, and whoever loses his life for My sake will find it" (Matt. 16:24-25). This is a paradox. But it is the paradox of Paradise.

Yes, let us deny ourselves, and confess Him. Let us confess Him for our own happiness. He tells us again today: "So every one who acknowledges Me before men, I also will acknowledge before My Father who is in heaven; but whoever denies Me before men, I also will deny before My Father who is in heaven." (Matt. 10: 32-33)

Let us confess Him that others may thereby be brought to Him. What he expected of Peter, He also expects of you tonight: "You shall be My witnesses" (Acts 1:8). To deny Him before men is to deny Him *to* men, to hide the Door to heaven from men.

But by our confession of Him we also *strengthen one another.* That is as it should be in the church. Looking ahead just prior to His denial, Jesus said to Peter: "Satan demanded to have you, that he might sift you like wheat, but I have prayed for you that your faith may not fail; and when you have turned again, *strengthen your brethren*" (Luke 22:31-32). Thus we, too, are to strengthen and encourage each other by our mutual witnessing to our Lord's power and love. Let's remember this: if the church is to be a power without, it must be strong within. Are you strengthening your brothers and sisters in the faith?

One last glance at the lonely, troubled figure in the courtyard. Fear moved Peter to try to make friends with the world that night. In a wider sense, you and I crave and seek recognition in this world. However, in the light of eternity is it not, after all, a small thing whether we are acknowledged by the world? Our chief aim in life is rather this: to confess our Lord faithfully, to be of help to one another, to stand with Him one day before the throne of His Father in heaven and receive His blessed commendation: "Well done, good and faithful servant . . . enter into the joy of your Master." (Matt. 25:21)

Lord, look on me as You once looked on Peter— before it is too late! Amen.

WERE YOU THERE

When He Was Accused?

Then the whole company of them arose and brought Him before Pilate. And they began to accuse Him, saying, "We found this man perverting our nation and forbidding us to give tribute to Caesar and saying that he himself is Christ a king." And Pilate asked Him, "Are you the King of the Jews?" And He answered him, "You have said so." And Pilate said to the chief priests and the multitudes, "I find no crime in this man." But they were urgent, saying, "He stirs up the people, teaching throughout all Judea, from Galilee even to this place."

LUKE 23:1-5

After His betrayal in the garden, the Lord was led away by His captors to the palace of the high priest. Here He was detained and humiliated in the quarters of Annas, the former high priest, until the Sanhedrin, the highest Jewish tribunal, could be called together. Soon the members of the council, who had been routed from their beds for this extraordinary and illegal session, were in their places. Under the scheming leadership of Caiaphas the high priest, Jesus was accused and condemned. And then "the whole company of them arose and brought Him before Pilate."

Let's take a brief look at this multitude. There are the

21

chief priests and elders, members of the Sanhedrin, and doubtless also some of their henchmen and hangers-on — possibly a hundred or more men. But because of the unique nature and deeper significance of the occasion the number is infinitely larger. In fact, the whole human race is rightly seen in this multitude which accused the innocent Christ. We shall see that we and all men share in that sin against the Lord. To sharpen our awareness of this tragic truth we put the question this evening:

WERE YOU THERE
WHEN HE WAS ACCUSED?

I

What were the accusations brought against Jesus?

Before the Jewish council the Lord was accused on religious grounds. It was difficult to find witnesses to testify against Jesus. But finally two false witnesses appeared who accused Him of having said something about destroying the great temple of Herod and rebuilding it again in three days. This was a distortion of a statement of Jesus concerning His death and resurrection on the third day. But the most serious charge was lodged against Him by the high priest Caiaphas, who in desperation abandoned his role as moderator and turned prosecutor. He drew from Jesus the blessed confession that He was the Son of God and for that accused Him of blasphemy, of insulting God. The Council then condemned Jesus to death — the penalty for blasphemy. Jesus was then hustled off to the headquarters of Pilate, for the Jews needed the sanction of the Roman government to carry out the death penalty.

However, before the governor Pontius Pilate, the

representative of the Roman government, the accusations are quite different. "And they began to accuse Him, saying, "We found this man perverting our nation and forbidding us to give tribute to Caesar and saying that he himself is Christ a king." Here the charges are based on alleged crimes against the state. We see how calculatingly the accusations are tailored to suit the occasion. That the charges were unjust and ridiculous need not be discussed. They were a combination of outright lies and half-truths. Even the Roman governor did not take them seriously. He was not deceived by this strange, sudden interest of the Jews in the welfare of the Roman state. And after briefly questioning Jesus about His alleged kingship, the governor flatly declared, "I find no crime in this man." As a matter of fact, these words become a refrain that is heard again and again throughout the trial of Jesus—indeed down through history.

The arraignment of the Holy One did not end with this trial before Caiaphas and Pilate. In the turbulent centuries which followed, down to this very day, the innocent Christ has been accused of many things. Some call Him a deceiver; others, a dreamer. Communism brands His blessed teachings as dangerous to the people.

But these charges and criticisms, today as then, collapse under the sheer weight of their own falseness. After all these years His standing challenge, "Which of you convicts Me of sin?" still silences maligning mouths (John 8:46). And those who are called upon to judge Him, and who like Pilate may not believe in Him or follow Him, are compelled to repeat the verdict of the Roman: "I find no crime in this man."

But we don't need that endorsement. We believe Him—believe Him because He has through the Gospel call spoken to us with an overpowering persuasiveness, as has no one else. He has fulfilled His promise to us, "You shall *know* the truth. . . . " This we have experienced.

II

Now let us look more closely at Jesus' accusers.

We see there first of all the chief priests, the elders, and other members of the Sanhedrin. These were personally and directly involved in these shameful accusations against the Son of God. But they do not stand alone. The sin of accusing God and His Son is a universal sin; it is a sin of all mankind.

Adam first accused God in the garden. After his violation of God's will, Adam accused God of having been responsible. Adam blamed not only Eve; he blamed God, too, when he said, "The woman whom *Thou* gavest to be with me, she gave me fruit of the tree, and I ate" (Gen. 3:12). Later on Job's wife accused God for their misfortune. She urged Job to curse God and die. During the wanderings of Israel in the wilderness the people whom God had miraculously led through the Red Sea and supplied with food, again and again accused God of having led them out of Egyptian bondage to rot in the wilderness.

Yes, the scene of the innocent Christ accused by the people of His day is the most tragic, but it is one of many incidents in which man has dared to accuse his Maker and his Redeemer.

The chief priests and the elders were there. Adam was there. The Israelites were there. Were you there — when Jesus was accused?

Have you ever felt, particularly during times of trouble or disappointment, that God isn't giving you a square deal? Have you ever prayed faithfully for something dear to your heart and then after waiting and waiting blamed God for not hearing your prayer? Do you ever feel that

Christ is asking far too much of you—of your time, of your talent, of your treasure? What is all this, if it is not accusing God and the Savior of being incompetent and unfaithful? And if we accuse God, in what way are we any different from those who unjustly accused His Son our Lord before the tribunal of Caiaphas and the court of Pilate? If we accuse God, then we were there with them.

We were there also because of our frequent offenses against the Eighth Commandment, "Thou shalt not bear false witness against thy neighbor." Whatever hurts our neighbor hurts God's Son. We cannot confine the implications of this word of God simply to courtroom witnessing. Luther explains it this way: "We should fear and love God that we may not deceitfully belie, betray, slander, nor defame our neighbor. . . ." For every person who has been falsely accused in court there are a thousand who have been slandered by malicious gossip over the bridge table, over cocktails, or over the back fence. Unfounded rumors and misinformation thoughtlessly repeated, and usually embellished, amount to slanderous accusations and are all part of that hideous sin which did not even spare the innocent Christ. And those who are always ready to lend a willing ear to these accusations are equally guilty.

Yes, if we are honest, we can't stand off tonight and simply condemn those who accused Jesus, but must rather confess an equal guilt and take our place among them.

III

But let us look once more at the Accused.

Whom do we see? An innocent man. Pilate condemned Him, but declared Him innocent. But more. He is the sinless Son of God. He, the accused and the judged, is

25

the Judge of all. As He stated before the high priest and the council: "Hereafter you will see the Son of Man seated at the right hand of power, and coming on the clouds of heaven" (Matt. 26:64). He is also the Savior of the world, as He said: "The Son of Man came not to be served but to serve, and to give His life as a ransom for many" (Matt. 20:28). It was His sinless, holy life that was laid on the scales to outbalance the weight of the world's sin —our sin.

All our heinous and damning sins of false accusation against God's Son and the sons of men have by His precious blood been wiped away. In God's beloved Son "we have redemption, the forgiveness of sins" (Col. 1:14). It is in the very righteousness of the Accused that the accusers find the righteousness with which to stand before God.

Behold, what manner of love God has bestowed upon us —once accusers of His Son—that we should be called the sons of God!

Knowing this, we can only look with horror upon the sin of false and loveless accusation in all its forms. Let us guard our minds and our lips that we speak no evil against our neighbor and so wound Christ anew. We can be content only with evermore striving to speak the truth and do the truth. Truth, God's truth, is the one thing we need most. That is the Great Indispensable of our lives. Let us be eternally grateful that we have this truth in Him who is the Way, the Truth, and the Life!

WERE YOU THERE

When He Was Condemned?

So when Pilate saw that he was gaining nothing, but rather that a riot was beginning, he took water and washed his hands before the crowd, saying, "I am innocent of this man's blood; see to it yourselves." And all the people answered, "His blood be on us and on our children!" Then he released for them Barabbas, and having scourged Jesus, delivered Him to be crucified.

MATTHEW 27:24-26

It is a terrible thing for a person to be condemned and sentenced to prison for a crime he did not commit. Even if the victim of a miscarriage of justice is later proved innocent and released from prison, the injustice cannot be completely undone. Even though the state makes some financial amends, nothing can restore the years of freedom lost in prison. It must be difficult for one who has been the victim of such injustice to keep from becoming implacably bitter.

In the text for this evening we see an even greater tragedy. This is the condemnation and sentencing to death, not merely of an innocent man, but of the sinless Son of God. Here was no ordinary case of mistaken justice, but a deliberate and calculated plot to thwart

27

justice. Our sense of honesty and fairness revolts at this sickening scene in the Roman praetorium.

But as we look more closely at the people involved in this shameful episode, we know that they do not stand alone. To some degree, all the motives and attitudes that we find at work there are still with us today — hatred, prejudice, false accusations, envy, dishonesty. These sins bind men of today to those men of 2,000 years ago. These things also raise their ugly heads in our hearts and lives. We must constantly battle to keep them under control. Therefore it is not out of place to ask

WERE YOU THERE
WHEN HE WAS CONDEMNED?

I

We observe that as Jesus only a short time before was condemned by the church, He is now condemned by the state.

Pilate, the Roman governor, admitted that it was within his arbitrary power to release or to crucify the innocent Christ. In spite of his better judgment, he chose to condemn an innocent man in order to save his own position. He was a politician in the bad sense of that term. With a pathetic show of right he washed his hands before the clamoring mob, saying, "I am innocent of this man's blood; see to it yourselves."

This was not the only instance in which Christ and His church have been condemned by the state. Others soon took Pilate's place. For 300 years the Roman emperors condemned Christ and His followers as persons dangerous to the state. The Christians were hunted down and put to death. The sands of the Roman arena ran red with the blood of these martyrs. In our own times atheistic communism has condemned Christ as dangerous, branding the Christian religion as well as others as "the opiate of the people." Christian altars have been desecrated, churches turned into museums and other public buildings, Christians persecuted and "liquidated." Other examples could be cited to show how in the course of history Pilate's sin, in essence, has been committed again and again.

We rightly abhor all condemnation of Christ by the state. But let us remember that we as Christians in America have a unique responsibility for our government. The relationship of church and state should of course be vitally important to all citizens, particularly to the Christians. If by indifference to our civic duties and responsibilities we permit government to fall into the hands of unscrupulous men so that justice, honesty, fairness, and truth are violated, are we not inviting and abetting the condemnation of everything Christ stands for? Will not the work of the church, the cause of Christ's kingdom, be made more difficult? In many ways, without our thinking, we may become guilty of condemning Christ and His cause, not so much by sins of commission as by sins of omission. In the end, however, is there any real difference?

The condemnation of our Lord by a representative of the Roman state should remind us that we cannot be content scrupulously to avoid condemning Christ. We should the more vigorously preach Him, confess Him in our lives as Christian citizens, and be ready to serve Him in public office, if we have the ability and opportunity.

II

But look again at the Biblical scene. We observe, furthermore, that Christ was condemned not only by an official of the state, but just as much by the people.

When Pilate hypocritically washed his hands of Jesus'

blood, the people shouted, "His blood be on us and on our children." A terrible thing to say! On Palm Sunday, a few days before, some of these people doubtless had acclaimed Him with Hosannas. What made them change? "The chief priests and the elders persuaded the people to ask for Barabbas and destroy Jesus" (Matt. 27:20). In their judgment of Jesus the people were influenced, prompted, goaded by others. Their mistake was that they let others do their religious thinking for them.

This is a common mistake. Jesus warns against it. Once when He asked His disciples, "Whom do men say that the Son of Man is?" He immediately followed with the question, "But who do you say that I am?" (Matt. 16:13, 15). We must know Him for ourselves. But our faith in Him, our thinking about Him, must be based on God's Word and not on man's. Some people are guided in their religious thinking by what prominent people think. If a scientist, movie star, philosopher, or explorer expounds the subject of religion, many people will go along with it because a very important person has said so. Well-meaning Christians sometimes adopt the same attitude. They believe what they do because their parents or church or pastor teach it. The teaching may be correct, but the teachers are not the ground of faith. Our religious thinking must be based solidly on God's Word. To build otherwise is to court disaster. Remember, the people in Pilate's court condemned Jesus because they let others do their religious thinking for them.

Furthermore, we see in this crowd another common human failing or sin. That is the inclination to judge and condemn our neighbor without just cause. How often don't we misjudge a person's remarks or actions and put the worst construction on them! Or how often don't we listen to prejudiced reports and then condemn! Jesus cautions us: "Judge not, and you will not be judged; condemn not, and you will not be condemned" (Luke 6:37). He knows what it is to be condemned by cold, loveless, misguided judgment. It was also this sin of man that added to His great suffering.

Can we honestly say that we have never had any part in these sins which were involved in the condemnation of our Lord? Surely our heart tells us we were there. It is only when we admit that we were there, that it was also for our sin that He suffered and died, that we can see Him as our Savior. It is only after we have acknowledged our sin and repented of our sin that we can say of Him, as Paul did, that He "loved *me* and gave Himself for *me*" (Gal. 2:20). This means that in Him, by His innocent suffering and death for the sin of all mankind, I too can find pardon and peace. By His condemnation He freed us from condemnation, so that there is now "no condemnation for those who are in Christ Jesus" and "who walk not according to the flesh but according to the Spirit." (Rom. 8:1, 4)

III

How can we explain the magnitude of God's grace in Christ? We of course cannot; we can only wonder at it. But our wonderment must soon give way to the question, Can't I somehow make amends for the sorrow and the pain that sin — my sin — has caused Him? The answer again is: No, *you* never can. *He* has made the atonement for that before God. For this we are forever indebted to Him.

But there are ways in which we can show our grateful love to Him. First, we can watch and pray that we do not in any way condemn Him anew. We can also be patient and forgiving toward those who criticize and judge us mistakenly and unjustly. General Robert E. Lee was once asked by the President what he thought of another officer called Whiting. "Whiting? Why, a very fine officer, Mr. President. One of the ablest men in the army," Lee replied. The President looked surprised. "But don't you know," he continued, "that General Whiting has been saying some very unkind things about you?" "Oh, yes," was the reply, "I knew that. But, Mr. President, you have asked me what I think of General Whiting, not what General Whiting thinks of me." The Christian, like his Lord, when he is reviled, will revile not again.

We can show our love to our Lord by defending those who are unjustly condemned and by speaking the truth one with another. This is the acid test of our love for Christ, namely, our Christian concern for others. No amount of tears over our sin and over the suffering it has caused Christ the Redeemer will mean anything if our love does not go out to those whom He redeemed and who are precious in His sight.

Let us this evening, as we see again the tragic spectacle of the innocent Christ condemned to death for our sins, ask His help to be more loyal to Him and to His church; to speak more boldly and positively in His behalf; and to defend our neighbor when he is unjustly condemned. For in this, too, His blessed word applies: "As you did it to one of the least of these My brethren, you did it to Me." (Matt. 25:40)

WERE YOU THERE

When He Was Crowned with Thorns?

Then the soldiers of the governor took Jesus into the praetorium, and they gathered the whole battalion before Him. And they stripped Him and put a scarlet robe upon Him, and plaiting a crown of thorns they put it on His head, and put a reed in His right hand. And kneeling before Him they mocked Him, saying, "Hail, King of the Jews!" And they spat upon Him, and took the reed and struck Him on the head.

MATTHEW 27:27-30

The text this evening reminds us of one of the most familiar paintings of the passion of our Lord, the *Ecce Homo*, showing Jesus wearing the crown of thorns. That painful crown platted by the soldiers and pressed into His sacred head has long since disappeared. But there have been others. Throughout the years men have been making their own crowns of thorns, sometimes not realizing what they were doing, and tormenting Christ anew with those crowns.

If this seems strange to you, then simply remember this, that the crown of thorns was just one of the instruments of torture which the soldiers used in their whole sordid game of mocking Christ. It was a symbol of their mocking attitude. And their mockery consisted in this:

33

to treat Jesus as a *king in name only*. That was the essence of their game. And that is the same treatment Christ gets today from so many. They regard him as their king in name only.

Is it possible that we, too, sometimes treat Him that way? Is it possible that we share in this shameful treatment of our Lord, in essence?

WERE YOU THERE
WHEN HE WAS CROWNED WITH THORNS?

I

Let us see what went on there. Pontius Pilate's soldiers — and some of them were no doubt the counterpart of our modern "goons" — had heard Jesus claim to be a king. Very well, then, they would now give Him the treatment that befitted such a king! For a king's garment, they put on Him a handy purple robe. For a crown of jewels, they placed on His head a crown of thorns. For a scepter, they put a reed in His hand. For loyal servants, they themselves bowed before Him, saying, "Hail, King of the Jews." Then they spit on Him, and took the reed and struck Him on the head.

Little did they realize what they were doing. Had they realized the truth, they would have paled with fear and trembled in terror. For He was King — the King of heaven and earth. The only-begotten Son of God left His heavenly kingdom to be born of the virgin in a stable in Bethlehem. He took upon Himself the form of a servant. But from time to time He gave the people glimpses of His almighty power. He stilled a storm at sea by the power of His word. He fed 5,000 people with the miracle of five barley loaves and two small fish. He called His dead friend Lazarus to life from the tomb where he had lain for four days. And now He had only a few hours before throwing to the ground those who had come to the garden to arrest Him. This was He whom these puny men were mocking and maltreating—the almighty God in the flesh.

Why, then, does He permit these coarse soldiers to mock Him and crown Him with thorns? The answer is that in these hours the Lord is not openly acting as King, but as Priest. He has laid aside the use of His kingly power in order to make an atonement for the sin of men, even of these men who are making this horrible sport of Him. As our Mediator before God, Jesus is about to bring a sacrifice for our sin, and that sacrifice is to be none other than His own spotless self. The reason why He endures these terrible indignities is that He is the Lamb of God who takes away the sin of the world. He is here fulfilling the prophecy of old: "He was wounded for our transgressions, He was bruised for our iniquities; upon Him was the chastisement that made us whole, and with His stripes we are healed. All we like sheep have gone astray . . . and the Lord has laid on Him the iniquity of us all." (Is. 53:5-6)

And if He was wounded for our transgressions, if by His stripes we were healed, then we were involved in His suffering, we contributed to it. For His suffering was caused by the sin of the human race, of which the sin of our age and of our lives is a part.

II

Were you there when He was crowned with thorns? Now let's see just what this was. This was all part of a more fundamental sin, that of treating Jesus as a king in name only. Don't we all fall into this sin at times? Let's not think here only of unbelievers and hypocrites. Let us think of ourselves who say we take Him seriously when He says: "My kingship is not of this world. . . . I am a king. For this I was born, and for this I have come into the world, to bear witness to the truth. Every one who is of the truth hears My voice." (John 18:36-37)

Our King says: "If you continue in My Word, you are truly My disciples, and you will know the truth, and the truth will make you free" (John 8:31-32). How much does God's Word figure in your daily life? Do you read it, study it? Is it important to you? If we neglect His Word, we despise and mock Him. He is not a king to us, but one whom we push aside. What of our attendance at public worship and our attendance at the Lord's Table? Don't we sometimes push Him aside here too? Don't we make of Him a king in name only?

Our King bids us love one another: "A new commandment I give to you, that you love one another; even as I have loved you, that you also love one another" (John 13:34). Yet there are those who call Jesus their king and who hate others, who carry long-standing grudges, and will not even talk to others. There are Christian homes which have on the walls plaques reading "Christ is the Head of this house, the Unseen Guest at every meal." But the discussion and strife that rules the hearts in that home show that Christ is there just a king in name only.

Or is Christ truly the King of our money and goods? Is He the King of our pocketbooks? If He were, then the church treasuries would be overflowing. There would not be any crippling deficits. If Christ were really and truly King to all in the area of Christian stewardship, there would be more and greater offerings of love to Him instead of what amounts to a mere tip now and then.

Our King urges us to be fervent in prayer. He says, "Whatever you ask in prayer, you will receive, if you have faith" (Matt. 21:22). Certainly, every Christian prays.

But don't we sometimes grow weak in prayer, pray half-heartedly or mechanically, as if it did not make any difference? That is to treat Jesus as a king in name only. All this is even more shameful in our case. The soldiers who knelt before Him admittedly did not take Jesus seriously as a king. But we say that we do.

Yes, we must admit we were there, and that we have been there again and again.

III

But in spite of all our sins of weakness against our King, in spite of our unworthiness, He forgives us by His grace and keeps us in His kingdom with Him. And He is able to do this because He has overcome all His enemies and our enemies. He reigns in glory now.

> The Head that once was crowned with thorns
> Is crowned with glory now;
> A royal diadem adorns
> The mighty Victor's brow.

Once He "emptied Himself, taking the form of a servant, being born in the likeness of men. And being found in human form He humbled Himself and became obedient unto death, even death on a cross. Therefore God has highly exalted Him and bestowed on Him the name which is above every name, that at the name of Jesus every knee should bow, in heaven and on earth and under the earth, and every tongue confess that Jesus Christ is Lord, to the glory of God the Father." (Phil. 2:7-11)

It was this glorification that Jesus foresaw even in the dark hours of His humiliation, and of which He prophesied: "Hereafter you will see the Son of Man seated at the right hand of power, and coming on the clouds of heaven." (Matt. 26:64)

It is this glorious coming to which we look forward with expectant joy. For by the power of His grace we, who have often placed a crown of thorns upon His sacred head, will then receive from His hands a crown of life. Then our hands, which have been cleansed by His precious blood, will be raised only in loving adoration and praise to our eternal Savior-King.

But until He comes in glory, let us serve Him more faithfully as our King in truth, not in name only. Let us praise and proclaim Him by word and deed that others may come to know Him as their Savior and King, that they may share His glory with us when He comes.

WERE YOU THERE

When He Was Crucified?

Two others also, who were criminals, were led away to be put to death with Him. And when they came to the place which is called The Skull (Calvary), there they crucified Him and the criminals, one on the right and one on the left. And Jesus said, "Father, forgive them; for they know not what they do." And they cast lots to divide His garments. And the people stood by, watching; but the rulers scoffed at Him, saying, "He saved others; let Him save Himself, if He is the Christ of God, His Chosen One!"

LUKE 23:32-35

During the quiet moments of these evening Lenten services we have followed our Lord step by step along the path of His great Passion for our sin. This evening the text brings us to the climax of His suffering, His crucifixion on Calvary.

Now the crucifixion of our Lord may be looked at in two ways: as the people saw it, and as Jesus saw it.

The text states: "The people stood by, watching." Most pictures of the crucifixion are painted from that point of view—the view of someone looking at the cross. But a few years ago a member of the University of Illinois department of art took the other point of view. He painted a picture, an extremely striking picture, of the scene on Calvary as it must have appeared to Jesus looking down from the cross. Although not many pictures have been done from this point of view, the text, significantly enough, does this very thing. It gives us Jesus' point of view as He looked down from the cross at the people: "Father, forgive them; for they know not what they do."

These words are the key to the understanding of Calvary. The crucifixion can be rightly understood by us only when we look at it from Jesus' point of view. It is the view of God's forgiving love. "Father, forgive them!" Whom did Jesus see when He spoke these words? Did He see you there?

WERE YOU THERE
WHEN HE WAS CRUCIFIED?

I

Jesus included all in His prayer for divine forgiveness. His eyes rested on the soldiers who had nailed Him to the cross. Now they were gambling for His clothing and His seamless coat, reminding us of the prophetic words of David in Psalm 22, "They divide My garments among them, and for My raiment they cast lots." No, they did not know what they were doing; they were hardened men, immune, no doubt, to human suffering; this was just another routine matter of Roman justice. But Jesus prayed that they might be forgiven.

From the cross Jesus could see the chief priests, scribes, and elders of the people. These were the ones who had plotted and engineered His crucifixion, and were as guilty as if they had hammered the nails into His hands and feet. Even now they still persist in their mockery and derision, "He saved others; let Him save Himself, if He is the Christ of God, His Chosen One!" again reminding us of the portentous words of Psalm 22. Although these religious leaders had certainly sinned against better knowledge, yet they really did not comprehend the enormity of their crime against the Son of God. Jesus prayed that they, too, might be forgiven.

Then Jesus could see the thieves crucified with Him, one on His left and the other on His right. Both of these criminals at first had ironically joined the chief priests in their jibes against Christ. But after a time the thief on the right, overcome by the strange power of the man on the center cross, repented. And Jesus spoke the word of pardon and peace to him.

And there were others who were not there personally, but whom the forgiving love of Jesus embraced in this prayer. Annas, Caiaphas, Pilate, Herod, Peter and the faithless disciples. He would forgive them too.

But the eyes of Jesus fell not only on His enemies beneath the cross. "Standing by the cross of Jesus were His mother, and His mother's sister, Mary the wife of Clopas, and Mary Magdalene. . . . and the disciple (John) whom He loved" (John 19:25-26). Were these His loved ones included in His prayer? After all, these brave souls had taken no active part in this tragedy. Their hearts were breaking with grief. But in the wider sense of Jesus' prayer for forgiveness, they too were included. For on the cross was not merely Mary's son, but God's Son, the only-begotten Son of God who had come into the flesh to redeem all mankind from sin. Behold the Lamb of God which taketh away the sin of the world!

And we who love Him today were there. Our sins helped put Him there. From the crest of Calvary the vision of the Crucified embraced us and all people, for we have all sinned and come short of the glory of God. Let us not be offended to hear this. Rather let us acknowledge our sin and thank Him for including us in His prayer for forgiveness. And ask His help to avoid sin, which once wounded Him and still wounds our fellowmen, especially the sin of refusing to forgive others. After being at Calvary with Jesus, can we refuse to give to others what He in His agony prayed His Father to give us? In His name let us, too, forgive.

II

There is another thing to remember here. Looking at the crucifixion from Jesus' point of view, we see that He not only prayed for our forgiveness but also died to *make this forgiveness a reality for us.*

What right does man have to expect God to be merciful to him? The Scripture says, "The soul that sins shall die" (Ezek. 18:20). Every man who honestly looks into his own soul will have to admit that he is a sinner, that he has in many ways transgressed the holy will of God. His conscience bears witness to this awful truth. But throughout the ages man has tried in hundreds of ways, both crude and refined, to make God favorable to him. The history of religion is for the most part the story of man's ceaseless efforts to placate outraged Justice, attempts of man to build a bridge or a ladder of his own that will lead him back into God's favor. But it is futile for man to try to lift himself out of the mire of his sin by his own bootstraps.

But Christ's view of His crucifixion is that *it* is the answer to mankind's yearning and striving to find peace with God, for by the merits of His own spotless life and of His innocent suffering and death He has paid our debt to God. For His crucified Son's sake God has canceled our sin. "It is finished!" This is the viewpoint of the Crucified as He looks out over the world from Calvary's cross: He hangs there to win forgiveness for them.

It is most important for us that we make Jesus' view of His crucifixion our own. The apostle Paul was one who understood this well. He had once been in the ranks of those who persecuted Christ and His church. By the forgiving grace of God he had in time been led to see the cross in its true meaning, as Jesus saw it. He saw Jesus hanging there for his sin. And this caused him to make a most striking confession, in which he saw himself not only among the vast number beneath the cross, but with Jesus *on* the cross. He said, "I have been crucified *with* Christ." Yes, Paul saw himself on the cross with Christ. This was not presumptuousness on his part, but rather the humble acceptance of the fact that Jesus bore his sin there. And that led Paul to continue: "It is no longer I who live, but Christ who lives in me; and the life I now live in the flesh I live by faith in the Son of God, who loved me and gave Himself for me." (Gal. 2:20)

This forgiveness which Christ won for us means new life for us today and every day. For those who have been with Jesus at Calvary, each new day means another day of God's forgiving love. Things may go wrong at home, in school, at work. Serious sickness or sorrow may come our way. Defeat may stare us in the face at every turn. Nevertheless, we live! If sin and sorrow and trouble are realities in our lives, then the power of God's forgiveness can be just as great, yes, a greater reality for us. It is the power of God's transforming love in our lives. God does not want you to be without it. He offers it again to you in Christ.

If we want to get the most out of this life and be assured of eternal life, we must first see ourselves crucified with Christ. We must realize that we were there, that we were not only beneath the cross, but *on* the cross with Him. You see, Christ died for the sins of the world, but only when we realize that *we* were there does He become *our* Savior.

> Bane and blessing, pain and pleasure,
> By the Cross are sanctified;
> Peace is there that knows no measure,
> Joys that through all time abide.

WERE YOU THERE

When He Gave the Holy Supper?

And He took bread, and when He had given thanks He broke it and gave it to them, saying, "This is My body which is given for you. Do this in remembrance of Me." And likewise the cup after supper, saying, "This cup which is poured out for you is the new covenant in My blood."

LUKE 22:19-20

This is the night in which the Savior was betrayed by one of His own disciples. But prior to this shameful scene the Scripture presents another picture which has become one of the most cherished by Christians of all times: the Last Supper.

The setting is a simple one. Twelve men and their Master are gathered together to observe the traditional Passover meal in an upper room somewhere in Jerusalem. It is the same scene as that being enacted in thousands of Jewish homes that very night.

The festival of the Passover was instituted by God at the time of the exodus of the Israelites from Egypt after four hundred years of slavery. According to God's instructions, the people on the day of their departure killed a lamb "without spot or blemish" and stained their doorways with its crimson blood. They roasted the lamb and

45

ate standing up, ready for travel. That night the avenging angel of God swept across the land of Egypt, leaving the firstborn of man and beast lifeless in his wake, but *passing over* the houses of the Israelites whose doorways were marked with the blood of the lamb. A once haughty but humbled Pharaoh now urgently pleaded with this troublesome people to leave with all haste. And six hundred thousand men, besides women and children, began their march to freedom.

God appointed this historic day as a memorial for them. The killing of the Passover lamb every year and the attendant ceremonies of the meal in each home were to be for all generations a vivid reminder of God's mighty deliverance.

This memorial meal it was which our Lord on that first Maundy Thursday was celebrating with His disciples in that upper room. Significantly, it was just during this last Passover meal that He instituted His Holy Supper of the new covenant in His blood, to replace that of the old. This is one of the most solemn and sublime moments of all time. Disciples could now enter into a communion with their Lord such as they had never before known. What a blessing for those who were there! Who were they? You recognize Peter, James, John, and the others. Any others? Look at the group again as Jesus saw it in His mind's eye. The Twelve become a multitude as they are joined at His table by countless other disciples down through the ages. What about you?

WERE YOU THERE
WHEN HE GAVE HIS HOLY SUPPER?

I

Jesus had you in mind in that upper room. This act,

like all the others of His great Passion, was also for you. He saw you there.

In the midst of the simplicity of the upper room you enter into a mystery of mysteries. At one point during the Passover supper Jesus takes bread, gives thanks, and gives it to His disciples, saying, "This is My body which is given for you. Do this in remembrance of Me." Then He takes the cup and gives it to them, saying, "This cup which is poured out for you is the new covenant in My blood." Behold, with the bread He gives His body and with the wine, His blood. This is the same body which in a short time will be nailed to the cross, the same blood which will be shed there *for them*, more specifically, as Matthew says, "for the forgiveness of sins." You do not know how this can be. But the Lord's own words assure you that when disciples eat of that bread and drink of that cup, they receive in a supernatural manner the true body and blood of their Lord.

This is to be done also in remembrance of Him. The perpetuation of His Holy Supper as a memorial until the end of time is also an assurance that Jesus has not only the Twelve in mind, but His disciples of all ages, also you. Those first disciples, especially, would need to remember His love and be reassured of His presence. For them there were most difficult days ahead. Jesus was about to withdraw His visible presence from them. What could He give them to support them as they went out into a bitterly hostile world to preach His Gospel of salvation? Nothing less than His own body and blood, which He gave and shed for them on the cross. This would always remind them, as it also reminds you, that His disciples do not stand alone in the world.

As you come to the Lord's Table this evening to commemorate His suffering and death for you, be assured once again that He thought also of you in the upper room when He gave His Holy Supper.

II

Because you were there in His thoughts, He also wants you to enjoy the blessings of His Supper in this your day. What these blessings are is contained in the message of the Lord's Supper.

That message is essentially nothing strange or new in His teaching. The Lord had told His disciples numerous times before, "The Son of Man came to seek and to save the lost" (Luke 19:10). Again, "The Son of Man came not to be served but to serve, and to give His life as a ransom for many" (Matt. 20:28). Again, "The Son of Man . . . must be killed, and after three days rise again" (Mark 8:31). Yes, all this He had patiently explained to them many times. And now, once more, He tells them that His body would be given and His blood would be shed for their sin. That is pure Gospel, the good news of forgiveness of sins through the death of Jesus Christ. That is the "new covenant" in His blood. But it is the same message, essentially, as that of the prophets of old who foretold His coming.

Although the message of the Gospel and of the Lord's Supper is one and the same, the Lord did add something in this Sacrament for you. In addition to His spoken promises, He now gives you a special pledge or guarantee of His forgiving love. It is nothing less than His own body and blood. We are familiar with the use of pledges. The wedding ring is a "pledge and token of wedded love and faithfulness." The precious body and blood of your Lord in the Sacrament is to be for you and all disciples until the end of time the unfailing token and pledge of His saving love. Then, too, as you personally receive the bread and the wine with your mouth, you understand more fully your Savior's words, "given and shed *for you*, for the remission of sins." In this Holy Supper, then, you have His boundless forgiveness *individualized* and *personalized*. It would mean little to you to know in an abstract way that God is Love. But it means everything to you to know that God loves *you*, that *you*, personally, sinner though you are, are the object and recipient of His saving love tonight.

The words, "This is My body, which is given for you . . . this is My blood, shed for you," also tell you that there is in this Supper a most blessed *communion* between you and your Lord and between you and your fellow communicants in the Lord. The Lord of heaven comes to you, is with you, in the eating and drinking of the earthly elements. "The cup of blessing which we bless, is it not a participation in the blood of Christ? The bread which we break, is it not a participation in the body of Christ?" says the apostle Paul (1 Cor. 10:16). Christ gives you this participation, this communion, for the strengthening of your faith in the forgiveness of your sins and for the furtherance of your Christian life. Therewith He also reinforces His great promise, "Lo, I am with you always, to the close of the age." (Matt. 28:20)

This blessed communion is yours because He had you in mind when He gave His Holy Supper.

III

Feast with your Lord again this evening and receive His blessings anew!

Many years have passed since that first Maundy Thursday, when the first disciples ate of that heavenly supper with their Lord. Since that time countless Christians throughout the ages have received the comfort and strength of this Holy Communion with their Lord and with each other in their own day. The Upper Room is ever a present-day room to the believer. When Leonardo da Vinci painted the *Last Supper,* he placed that incident from the life of our Lord into a contemporary setting. Under the magic of his brush, the Upper Room becomes an Italian dining hall. The Master and His disciples take their places at a Renaissance table. Tonight, as we are gathered here to eat and to drink with Him, this twentieth-century church is transformed into the Upper Room. The same Host is here. Disciples are here. You are among them. You hear His words, "This is My body, which is given for you. . . . My blood, which is shed for you. . . . "

For you! How grateful you should be for those words! We acknowledge and confess our sins and shortcomings as God's children. You know best what your sins are, as a parent, a neighbor, a son or daughter, a student, an employer, an employee. If it were not for the earnest invitation of your Lord and His precious promise of pardon and peace in this Sacrament, you might well hesitate to come before Him, for fear that a just and holy God might turn His face from you. But can you doubt the words of Him who gave His own body and shed His own blood to make all things right for you with God? Must not your grateful heart sing with St. Paul: "Therefore, since we are justified by faith, we have peace with God through our Lord Jesus Christ. Through Him we have obtained access to this grace in which we stand, and we rejoice in our hope of sharing the glory of God" (Rom. 5:1-2). Again, "For you did not receive the spirit of slavery to fall back into fear, but you have received the spirit of sonship. When we cry, "Abba! Father!" it is the Spirit Himself bearing witness with our spirit that we are children of God, and if children, then heirs, heirs of God and fellow heirs with Christ, provided we suffer with Him in order that we may also be glorified with Him." (Rom. 8:15-17)

One of the bitter experiences of life is the experience of being rejected. One can take many kinds of blows, but to be rejected by one's fellowmen is indeed staggering. It is something for which no amount of money or influence or education can compensate. You are a social being, created so by God. Acceptance by your fellowman is vital to your happiness. But much more important—no, all-important—is your acceptance by God. There is no anguish more haunting than the feeling of being rejected by God. For that, my friends, is hell!

Jesus, your Lord, experienced both rejections. He was despised and rejected by men. He was forsaken by God. But it was precisely through His terrible rejection that you are accepted. Never need you be haunted by the tormenting thought that God does not want you.

You were there in His thoughts when He gave His Holy Supper. Thank and praise Him all your days for that. For the solid bedrock of your hope and joy are these words: "This is My body which is given for *you*. . . . This cup which is poured out for *you* is the new covenant in My blood. Do this in remembrance of Me." Amen.

WERE YOU THERE

When He Was Laid in the Tomb?

After this Joseph of Arimathea, who was a disciple of Jesus, but secretly, for fear of the Jews, asked Pilate that he might take away the body of Jesus, and Pilate gave him leave. So he came and took away His body. Nicodemus also, who had at first come to Him by night, came bringing a mixture of myrrh and aloes about a hundred pounds' weight. They took the body of Jesus, and bound it in linen cloths with the spices, as is the burial custom of the Jews. Now in the place where He was crucified there was a garden, and in the garden a new tomb where no one had ever been laid. So because of the Jewish day of Preparation, as the tomb was close at hand, they laid Jesus there.

JOHN 19:38-42

How does one go about describing that tremendous moment in history when the Son of God died on the cross for the sin of the world?

Perhaps it were better for us not to attempt any such thing, better simply to turn to the plain and reverent language of the inspired record: "Then Jesus, crying with a loud voice, said, 'Father, into Thy hands I commit My spirit!' And having said this, He breathed His last." (Luke 23:46)

All was finished now—not only His suffering of the last few hours, but everything He had come to do. It began in God's heart in eternity. It began on earth in the manger, on a silent starlit night, the night the angel told the shepherds—and the world, "Be not afraid; for behold, I bring you good news of a great joy which will come to all the people; for to you is born this day in the city of David a Savior, who is Christ the Lord" (Luke 2:10-11). Strangely enough, it was gloriously completed on a cross—the work of man's redemption—on a day as dark as night. No angel voices are heard here. Only His voice. It is fitting that He, the dying yet triumphant Son of God, Himself should make the announcement of His victory: "It is finished!" (John 19:30)

His soul now rested in His Father's hands. His bruised and lifeless body still remained on the cross. The leaders insisted that the bodies be removed before the Sabbath, which was a high day. It would not be a pretty sight for the pilgrims and visitors who had overflowed Jerusalem for the Passover. So the legs of the two thieves were clubbed to hasten their death. But this was not necessary in Jesus' case. He was already dead. To make sure, a soldier jabbed a spear into His side. But the Lord had by an act of His will laid down His life, as He had foretold. Now, what would happen to His body? This was the question that must have filled the already tortured minds of that loyal little band standing beneath the cross. We can perhaps feel something of their anxiety at a time like this.

An understanding God has preserved for us in the Sacred Record a moving and thoroughly human story of the burial of our Lord. It is the story of loving hands that gently laid to rest His pierced and pallid body. The artist Rubens and others have endeavored to recapture on canvas the moment of the descent from the cross. It is a picture of outstretched hands, willing and helpful hands, which received His body and bore it to the tomb. But many other people were there who could not possibly be included in such a picture — for example, you and I.

WERE YOU THERE
WHEN HE WAS LAID IN THE TOMB?

I

There is Joseph of Arimathea, a respected and well-to-do man. Joseph was a member of the Jewish council, the Sanhedrin, which had condemned Jesus to death, but he had not consented to the deed. He was a devout man, waiting for the appearance of the Messiah. In fact, he was a disciple of Jesus, but "secretly, for fear of the Jews" (v. 38). Somehow he has overcome his fear and now goes boldly to Pilate to ask for the body of Jesus. He wants to give His body a decent burial in his own family tomb, a new tomb, where nobody had yet been laid. Having received the governor's permission, Joseph saw to it that the body of Jesus was removed from the cross. Now, all this was a public confession on the part of Joseph as to his relation to the crucified One. By this action he threw off the cloak of secrecy. He was willing to stand up and be counted. And what a joy this must have been for the brave women and that disciple John, who out of love for their crucified Lord had faced the abuse and scorn of the mob alone. Through this new ally their Lord's body would be reverently cared for and given honorable burial.

Then there is Nicodemus, another member of the Sanhedrin. You will recognize him as the one who came to Jesus by night because he was either ashamed or afraid to be seen in the company of the Nazarene. That was a memorable visit — perhaps there had been others — when he learned from Jesus the true nature of the kingdom of God and how to enter it: "Unless one is born of water and the Spirit, he cannot enter the kingdom of God. That which is born of the flesh is flesh, and that which is born of the Spirit is spirit. Do not marvel that I said to you, 'You must be born anew'" (John 3:5-7). Certainly Nicodemus had not consented to the death of Jesus; perhaps he had not been present when He was condemned. At any rate, he cannot remain a secret disciple any longer. Nicodemus now comes out into the open. He approaches the garden tomb, bringing a supply of costly spices, a mixture of myrrh and aloes, for embalming the body. Again, what joy his coming must have brought to the friends of Jesus, as they now saw that in the end their Lord would receive a decent burial.

Is there anything we can learn from these men? Certainly not from their former fear, which caused them to hide their light under a bushel. But there is something here for those who faithfully "stand beneath the cross," in the thick of things alone. Sometimes they may get to feel like Elijah of old, lonely and beaten. It seemed to him that everyone in Israel, man, woman, and child, had forsaken God and had turned to worship Baal. In his discouragement he lamented to God, "I, even I only, am left" (1 Kings 19:14). That was probably true so far as Elijah could see at the moment. But God, the Searcher of hearts, reminded His dejected servant that He had yet seven thousand in Israel who had not bowed the knee to Baal. Elijah saw only himself; God discerned thousands of others. Yes, the church of God is much, much bigger than we sometimes think. The seven thousand in Israel and the Josephs and the Nicodemuses remind us of that today. Remind us that there is a church in Red China, that there is a church in Soviet Russia, in the hearts in which the Crucified dwells. Remind us of the lines from the mission hymn:

> Who dare not yet the faith avow,
> Tho' secretly they hold it now.

Remind us that God, at His hour, can embolden all of them to step forth and confess Him openly before the world.

II

The once timid Joseph and Nicodemus come forward to join the others who had stood beneath the cross — drawn together in the world by that cross. Together their hands prepare the body of their Lord. See them gently lift the body and carry it into Joseph's tomb and then roll a heavy stone before the entrance.

Yet not their hands alone laid Him in the tomb. Their hands were the hands of the world — your hands and my hands. We, too, helped lay Him there. It was our sin that laid Him, God's incarnate Son, into the grave. You need but recall that for His own sake God's Son had no need to suffer and to die and be buried. You must know, therefore, that in all this He was taking the place of others, acting as their Substitute. This is stated many times and in many ways in the Scripture. Thus Paul writes to the Colossian Christians: "And you, who once were estranged and hostile in mind, doing evil deeds, He has now reconciled in His body of flesh by His death, in order to present you holy and blameless and irreproachable before Him" (Col. 1:21-22). He could do this because He, the Son of God, also became one of us and lived among us. He lived a life of perfect obedience to God's holy will. We had transgressed that will and deserved to die. He took upon Himself our punishment, died for us, made an atonement for us.

So, then, we face this startling paradox: we say that we helped to lay Christ in Joseph's tomb, and we say that at the same time we were carried into the tomb with Him. Both statements are gloriously true. How so? Our sin, for which He died, put Him there. And since it was our sin which He took with Him into the tomb, we also went in with Him. When the stone was sealed on Him, it was also sealed on us. This is what St. Paul was talking about when he wrote to the Christians in Rome: "We were buried with Him." Indeed, it is only "if we have been united with Him in a death like His" that we can come forth again and "be united with Him in a resurrection like His." (Rom. 6:4-5)

Our Lord's burial is significant, furthermore, because it is another confirmation of His death for us. Again, His burial fulfills a pointed prophecy of Isaiah in connection with the Messiah's death, namely, "They made His grave with the wicked and with a rich man in His death" (Is. 53:9). Thus even in the point of the burial of our Lord we find the evidence of divine direction. Finally, His burial marks the last stage in His state of humiliation before His glorious exaltation on the third day.

III

It is of the utmost personal importance for you to understand that you were there when they laid Him in the tomb, that your sins were buried with Him. For to know and gratefully accept what He has done for you means to share in the eternal blessings of His death and resurrection. To those who are in fellowship with Him the grave becomes something quite new. It is not an end, but a beginning; not a blank wall, but an open door.

So it is that when we stand at the tomb of a fellow believer, a loved one, we know the grief and sorrow that all must feel at such a time, but with a tremendous difference. It is that difference which Christ alone makes, the difference expressed in the immortal words of St. Paul: "We would not have you ignorant, brethren, concerning those who are asleep, that you may not grieve as others do who have no hope. For since we believe that Jesus died and rose again, even so, through Jesus, God will bring with Him those who have fallen asleep." (1 Thess. 4:13-14)

Not all who die are buried by loving hands. The victims of war, of concentration camps and purges, are often literally "plowed under" with a terrible machinelike precision. Yet it is really not important what the hands of man may do for or to our lifeless forms. What matters is what Christ did for us when He once shared the grave with us.

Some graves in this vast cemetery of the earth bear no identification. No man knows who rests there. In Arlington National Cemetery is the well-known Tomb of the Unknown Soldier. This monument is a symbol of all the unknown dead. But they are unknown only to us. God knows them — each one of them. And the Good Shepherd who gave His life for the sheep reminds us: "My sheep hear My voice, and I know them, and they follow Me; and I give them eternal life, and they shall never perish, and no one shall snatch them out of My hand." (John 10:27-28)

Yes, this is why He died for us. This is why He hallowed the grave for us. This then is the mighty affirmation of Good Friday: "O death, where is thy victory? O death, where is thy sting? The sting of death is sin, and the power of sin is the Law. But thanks be to God, who gives us the victory through our Lord Jesus Christ" (1 Cor. 15:55-57). This alone is what makes it a *Good* Friday for us. Amen.

WERE YOU THERE

When He Rose from the Grave?

We were buried therefore with Him by baptism into death, so that as Christ was raised from the dead by the glory of the Father, we too might walk in newness of life. For if we have been united with Him in a death like His, we shall certainly be united with Him in a resurrection like His.

ROMANS 6:4-5

We take our place this morning with millions of worshipers the world over, from the historic Holy Land to the colorful Grand Canyon. We have come together to celebrate the decisive victory of our Lord over death and the grave. By this we mean that Jesus Christ, the Son of God, who was crucified under Pontius Pilate, whose lifeless body was sealed in Joseph's tomb, on the third day snapped the bonds of death and rose victoriously from the grave.

Of all the events in the life of our Lord, His glorious resurrection is undoubtedly the one we should like most to have witnessed. What an overwhelming experience it would have been to stand before the empty tomb, to hear the angel's message, to talk with those Roman guards!

There is, however, a greater privilege than that of having been present at the resurrection as a mere spectator. It is the privilege of having been involved in the resurrection as a participant and beneficiary. But is such a thing possible? What do you think?

WERE YOU THERE
WHEN HE ROSE FROM THE GRAVE?

Remember, Christ was your heaven-sent Substitute. The text tells you that when on Good Friday He died for your sins, it was as though you had died. When on Easter morning He victoriously rose from the grave, it was as if you had risen to life again. The text reminds you that through your Baptism you participate in the death and resurrection of your Lord and share in their great blessings. In Christ you were there!

Consider this morning the deep personal significance this Easter truth holds for you.

I

The resurrection affirms and confirms the deity of your Lord.

Jesus on numerous occasions had predicted His death on the cross. What is more significant is the fact that He likewise foretold His resurrection. He said not only that "the Son of Man will be delivered into the hands of men, and they will kill Him" but also that "after three days He will rise" (Mark 9:31). No mere mortal could seriously make such a claim. God alone has the power over death. God alone is the Source of life, yes, is Life. When Jesus asserted that He would rise from the grave, He was claiming for Himself the power over death, the possession of life itself. He was claiming to be God. And when He burst forth alive from the tomb, He proved it.

Do not permit any Easter pageantry or music or

oratory to becloud this first great affirmation of the resurrection, namely, that it was God Himself who burst forth from the darkness of Joseph's tomb that first Easter day.

This is a tremendous affirmation. It means that the resurrected Christ is the Truth—"the Way, the Truth, and the Life." It means He is the omnipotent Lord of life and death. Our Savior Christ Jesus "abolished death, and brought life and immortality to light through the Gospel." (2 Tim. 1:10)

Friend, are you one who feels that he has been mocked in his search for the truth? Are you disillusioned and cynical because you have come to feel that life really has no meaning? Let me remind you once again, in the light of the resurrection, of the Savior's familiar words: "Come to Me, all who labor and are heavy laden, and I will give you rest. Take My yoke upon you, and learn from Me; for I am gentle and lowly in heart, and you will find rest for your souls" (Matt. 11:28-29). If on this Easter morning some disturbing problem of everyday living is robbing you of your joy, remember His words, "Seek first His kingdom and His righteousness, and all these things shall be yours as well" (Matt. 6:33). You've heard these words many times. But this morning I ask you to consider them in the resplendent light of Easter. Behind those words is not merely a kindly teacher, but the Son of God who showed to the world His truth and His power when He broke forth from the tomb. What we need most today is not more admiration of Jesus Christ, but *adoration* of this Christ as the Son of God, the Source of all truth and power. We need a day-by-day faith in His promises to help.

> Faith is the grasping of Almighty Power,
> The hand of man laid on the arm of God;
> That grand and blessed hour

In which the things impossible to me
Become the possible, O Lord, through Thee.

Victorious living is possible for those who are risen with Christ. It is part of that glorious walking "in newness of life."

II

The second great affirmation of the resurrection is that of your complete redemption from sin by your victorious Lord.

Man needed desperately to be redeemed because he had sinned against God. Sin is a dreadful reality. If you believe in God, you must believe in sin; for "sin is lawlessness" (1 John 3:4 RSV), "transgression of the law" of God (KJV). You cannot eliminate sin from your life by denying it or "soft-pedaling" it. "A well-known preacher was once taken to task by one of his hearers for preaching a pointed sermon on sin. His well-meaning critic stated that if people heard so much about sin they would become sinners. The preacher took a bottle marked 'poison' from a shelf. 'I see what you want me to do,' he said. 'You want me to change the label. Suppose I take off this label and put on a mild label, like "essence of peppermint." Do you see what happens? The milder you make the label, the more dangerous you make the poison.'"

Sin is so dangerous because it alienates you from your God. You cannot live apart from God. "The wages of sin is death" (Rom. 6:23). "Sin came into the world through one man and death through sin, and so death spread to all men because all men sinned." (Rom. 5:12)

Sin is so dangerous because it alienates you from your fellowman. Sin keeps you from composing your differences with others. In war as well as in your more personal

62

relationships, the destructive and corrosive nature of pride, jealousy, duplicity, suspicion, hatred, and moral ignorance plays the major role, but is not fully recognized.

Now, the central message of the cross is that Jesus Christ, the Son of God, suffered and died in behalf of the sinful human race. He was your God-sent Substitute who took your guilt upon Himself, who suffered to pay the penalty of your sin. On the cross, when His work of redemption was complete, He cried out, "It is finished!" But was it finished? Would His death suffice for us? Did He accomplish our redemption before God? During the dark hours between that Black Friday and that first Easter day, these questions remained unanswered. Then, on the first day of the week the answer came in a flashing, blinding light, bursting from the tomb upon the world: "He is risen!"

That is the victory in which you share. Listen, Paul tells the believers at Rome, and all believers: "We were buried therefore with Him by baptism into death, so that as Christ was raised from the dead by the glory of the Father, we too might walk in newness of life."

"O death, where is thy victory? O death, where is thy sting? The sting of death is sin, and the power of sin is the Law. But thanks be to God, who gives us the victory through our Lord Jesus Christ" (1 Cor. 15:55-57). Yes, God says to you through the resurrection of His Son: "Be sure, My child, your redemption from sin and death and hell is complete."

Accept your redemption from His holy hands. Thus you enter into new life with Him and "know the power of His resurrection" in your life. This is a transforming power. Every Christian has experienced it. It is freedom from an accusing conscience once at war with God. It is assurance of peace with God in Christ, that peace "which passes all understanding." It is not the release from the suffering, the pain, and the sorrows of life. But it is the resource with which to face them, endure them, in a victorious way. Here is power also — in the forgiving love of God — to better our relationships with one another in our everyday lives. I am sure you will agree, for example, that a husband and wife who have taken the Christ of Easter into their hearts by faith and who regularly pray together for His daily blessing will have a much happier homelife. I am also sure that those who sincerely pray His prayer, including "forgive us our trespasses, as we forgive those who trespass against us," are not likely to harbor bitterness and resentment — things which so often disturb relationships at home, at work, at school, in the neighborhood, and even in the congregation.

Open your heart so that the cleansing and ennobling light of the resurrection may shine in with a newer brilliance. It is the Lord's earnest desire that you live in the light of your assured redemption, that you "walk in newness of life."

III

Now, as you look once more toward the empty tomb, the third great affirmation of the resurrection of your Lord is brought home to you: the resurrection of your body through Him. Paul says in the text: "For if we have been united with him in a death like His, we shall certainly be united with Him in a resurrection like His." (V. 5)

The idea of the continuation of life after death is nothing new. The pagans, among them Socrates and Plato, believed in existence beyond the grave. The disciples of Jesus, crushed in spirit as they were, presumably had no doubts concerning their Master's immortality. But the resurrection of the body is a distinctive doctrine of the

Christian religion. Jesus often referred to the subject. Once He said, "This is the will of My Father, that every one who sees the Son and believes in Him should have eternal life; and I will raise him up at the last day" (John 6:40). Later, St. Paul, referring to the resurrection of the body, wrote to the Thessalonians: "But we would not have you ignorant, brethren, concerning those who are asleep, that you may not grieve as others do who have no hope. For since we believe that Jesus died and rose again, even so, through Jesus, God will bring with Him those who have fallen asleep." (1 Thess. 4:13-14)

All this, again, has substance and meaning only because of the actual resurrection of our Lord from the dead. In Him you have more than the promise of an uncertain existence in some shadowy spirit world. In Him you have the certainty of personal and bodily identity beyond the grave. This is also the basis of the comforting Christian hope of the recognition of loved ones in His Kingdom of Glory.

Life in His kingdom must begin here and now for you. In fact, you must possess it now, if you are to enjoy it in its fullness when He comes again. This should not be surprising. For in Him the here and the hereafter are joined in an unbroken, never-ending present. God wants you to enter His kingdom now through faith in the risen Savior. That is why He has given you Easter with its great affirmations: the deity of your Lord, your complete redemption by your Lord, and your bodily resurrection through your Lord.

The angel's message is once more resounding through the world: "He is not here; He is risen!" By Holy Baptism you were there when He rose from the grave. You now have the assurance that you will also be there when He returns in glory. Therefore, lift up your voice with all the redeemed in the mighty, swelling chorus, "Thanks be to God, who gives us the victory through our Lord Jesus Christ!"

But, friend, now that you have all this, what are you going to do with it? Amen.

THE SIGN OF THE CROSS —

THE SIGN

of Forgiveness

And Jesus said, "Father, forgive them; for they know not what they do." And they cast lots to divide His garments.

LUKE 23:34

One of the strange, mysterious marks of the church of the twentieth century is the fact that between Ash Wednesday and Easter Sunday morning there will be more people in the churches of Christendom than at any other time of the year. In order to understand this more clearly, it becomes necessary to examine these crowds more closely. Essentially there are three groups in our churches during the season of Lent. First, there are those who will be there also in July and August—the steady, quiet saints who are the glory of the kingdom of God on earth. Second, there are those who are in church during Lent by custom and tradition. They have learned from their childhood that this is a good time to be in church. Actually, it does not mean very much except that they catch a glimpse of the faith of their childhood. Third, there are those who are somehow haunted by the gallant figure of the lonely Sufferer on the cross. Their minds, cut by the acids of modernity, have succumbed to a vague, uneasy feeling that He knew something which life and time have taken away from the world. They see in Him a relentless strength, a far hope, and a continuing dream of goodness which the modern world has so largely forgotten.

All these people, however, have one purpose in common. They have come to see a man die. There is a strange fascination about this. Death is the one universal and inevitable experience. Further, the human race has discovered that we can learn how to live by practice. Each experience, whether it be happy or tragic, will, if we are wise, teach us something about the next. For the supreme experience of death, however, life furnishes no rehearsal. We can learn only by walking to the last door with others, by listening to their dying words and carrying them in remembering hearts for the day when we, too, shall join the majority of the wise and the silent.

We, too, have come to this church to see a man die. Even humanly speaking, He is one of the great figures of life and history. Even the most hardened unbeliever will admit that He changed the course of history. His dying words, therefore, must be tremendously and enormously important.

Seven times He spoke, three times to men, three times to God, and once to Himself.

The first word from the cross — "Father, forgive them; for they know not what they do" — is totally unexpected. He says nothing about Himself. Like lightning our Lord's first words strike straight into the heart of all the tragedy of mankind. The face under the crown of thorns goes up. The marching years become the accompaniment of His words, and the crowd around the cross is transformed into the human race. The world hears a dying man point to the reason for death: "Father, forgive them; for they know not what they do."

Surely this is no sudden thought without a long background and without a profound cause. This word reaches far back beyond the centuries into the quiet unbroken calm of eternity, where there was only God. It reaches back into the counsels of the Holy Trinity, where there was the vision of the cross against the darkened sky and the far silhouette of those torn and lifeless arms. It reaches back into the garden in the cool of the day when Adam and Eve were hiding from the voice of God after the fall into sin. It reaches back into all the voices of the prophets and kings who had said something about this dying Man on the cross. It reflects the quiet night when there was a Child born in a stable at Bethlehem. It reminds us of the words of our Apostolic Creed: "born of the Virgin Mary, suffered under Pontius Pilate, was crucified, dead, and buried."

This now was the fulfillment of all these events. It was Friday forenoon. A crowd poured out of the Damascus Gate. This was the climax of the drama of redemption. Now God could do no more. His infinite love for mankind was now reflected most clearly in the person, the work, and the words of His only-begotten Son dying on the cross. This first word is, therefore, for all our yesterdays and all our tomorrows. It is not only for those who are standing there but for all men who have lived and will live. It picks up all the years and rolls them up to heaven for the forgiveness of our heavenly Father.

There are few words in Holy Writ which more clearly point to the tremendous, dark, and tragic fact of sin. It is necessary for us today to stay with this thought for a moment. There are some things we can do about sin. We can be sorry for it. We can regret it. We can weep over it. We can offer to make reparation when our sin has struck someone else. There is, however, one thing we cannot do about sin. We cannot forgive it. Someone has to go the long rest of the way. There must be a voice from the cross against the long silence of eternity, over the noise of two thousand years, "Father, forgive them; for they know not what they do."

"For they know not what they do!" We have all heard the agonized question: What is really wrong with the world and the human race? Here is the great answer: moral stupidity! There is a stupidity of the mind and a stupidity of the soul, and nothing in the world is more terribly fatal than the latter. After all, who crucified Jesus Christ? Men too blind to see who He was, too dull to hear the truth, too stupid to care about goodness and holiness and truth. How often has every faithful pastor heard the words, usually spoken in bitter tears: "If I had only known—what would happen with that careless word of mine, with my turning away from my friend, with my momentary anger or passion!" "If I had only known"—this is often the moral epitaph for a situation which can never be remedied by human thought or human effort.

And yet the tremendous, mysterious thing about this prayer is that it points to this moral stupidity as the basis for our Lord's plea for our forgiveness. "They know not what they do." They think that they are wise, intelligent, and shrewd—but, My heavenly Father, they are children. They are bad and wicked children. They do not know to what end their deeds finally lead. They do not have the imagination; they do not have the moral insight. Let it be said again, as it has been said these many hundreds of years, that sin is always unintelligent, stupid, and foolish. It always ends in the ashes of burned-out fires and the gray dust of shame.

All this is no faraway story or a lost and broken dream. This is the past, present, and future sign of the forgiveness of the cross. Certainly all of us need this as we need nothing else. We have brought memories into this church of our own sins over the years. These memories burn. There are things that we should like to forget. The great, holy, and blessed thing about the sign of forgiveness is that a preacher can now stand up and under the sign of the cross give you this forgetfulness. There can be a drying of our tears over our sins. There can be relief from the tearing pain in our hearts. There can be a return to heaven and hope. "Father, forgive them; for they know not what they do." We may be children crying in the night, stupid, willful, and wrong, but we are still His children. By His grace we can now promise that we will try to do better. We can come to His cross in penitence and faith. If we do that, suddenly He is high and lifted up; and the age-old beautiful story of the Prodigal Son is reenacted again and again in this church and all over the world.

When that happens by the grace and mercy of God, then there is also a second lesson we can learn from this word. Every day we pray: "Forgive us our trespasses as we forgive those who trespass against us." No amount of twisting and turning can get away from this fact: We are asking for forgiveness in the measure in which we are ready to forgive — no more and no less. We are tying our life to the life of God in Jesus Christ. It is therefore completely wrong to say, "I can forgive, but I cannot forget." By the grace of God we can do what God has done for us. We can also forget. He has forgotten our sins. He has buried them in the bottomless sea of His eternal pity. So we are to act in our realm, in our little life, as God acts in all life and history. Even though our time is so short and our way together so brief, we must find time to forgive and forget the trespasses and sins of others. There is no sense in staggering toward eternity with a heavy burden of grudges and hurts and jealousy and hate and malice.

72

"Forgive us — as we forgive." This is one of the great signs of the cross. This is God's way of doing things. It is the way of incredible power. It reflects a love that will not let go. It shows us again a love which bears all things for us.

Finally, there is no way in which the human heart can ignore this basic lesson of the cross. It is true, of course, that sometimes men do not see the divine way — the way of forgiveness, of love and gentleness and humility. They feel that there are better ways of solving the deep and dark problems of the human heart. It is, therefore, necessary also for our generation to turn again and again to the sign of the cross. This way is always up. It leads finally beyond the flaming ramparts of our world to a world where there will at long last be no need of forgiveness and where we shall finally know, by His grace and mercy, what we are doing. We shall see very clearly that the ultimate power lies not in hate and fear and force but in forgiveness and love and grace. This is the sign of the cross.

THE SIGN

of Peace

"Peace I leave with you; My peace I give to you; not as the world gives do I give to you. Let not your hearts be troubled, neither let them be afraid."

JOHN 14:27

More than fifty years have come and gone since America paused for a moment to bury in Arlington National Cemetery the body of the Unknown Soldier of World War I. Lost and forgotten in life, he was to become in death a perpetual symbol of the world's hope and a silent messenger of the world's peace. Near his tomb men placed an eternal light so that his memory might live in the grateful hearts of his countrymen. Today, fifty years later, the dim and grim shadow of irony surrounds that light. Certainly we do not live in a world of peace. Today, fifty years after the body of this unknown soldier found its last resting place, it looks as though he had died in vain. The world is haunted with fear, and the horizons of humanity are red with blood.

It is therefore vitally necessary for us to turn again and again to an old and yet ever new peace. It is interesting to note how often our Lord used that little word, how often it appears in the story of His visit with us from Bethlehem to the final hill in Galilee, how it rings like a tolling bell especially through His Maundy Thursday sermon and His high-priestly prayer. "Peace I leave with you"—this is finally the end of all He said and did for us. This is what He wanted us to have by His obedient life and atoning death.

Today we may well pause to inquire into the reasons for the world's loss of God's peace. Why do men hate one another? Why do the councils of the great of the earth calmly proceed to plan the killing of their fellowmen? To answer these questions in terms of the demands for trade and territory, in terms of the personality of our leaders, in terms of the lust for power, does not strike at the heart of our problem. The answer is at the same time deeper and simpler than that! If you go out into nature at dusk, you will find that trees, stones, and hills cast shadows which are out of all proportion to the realities of the world and which will give you, if you attend only to them, a grotesque and utterly unreal picture of the realities behind these shadows. Something like that happens in the history of men with fearful regularity. Under the accumulated burden of fear upon fear and shame upon shame the eyes of men turn down and down and deeper down until they see only the shadows of the realities of God—the shadows which persuade them that momentary panaceas and temporary plans and endless conferences are going to heal the world's pain and turn away the world's ruin. There is no permanent hope in this. All the history of men and all the experience of the human heart are against it. You cannot heal a cancer by covering it with bandages. You cannot remove hate and fear and despair from the heart of the world by conducting some summit conferences. You may postpone their final result. But the realities are still here: the old envies, the old vanities, the old fears, the stark and grim reality of the sin-stricken heart of man—

man who will hate and destroy and kill because there is no peace in his own heart.

Our Lord therefore speaks this Lenten season with particular force to the heart of the modern world: "Peace I leave with you, My peace I give unto you; not as the world giveth, give I unto you." There is the answer—the only answer which can stand up in the light of eternity. This is the peace which our Lord fills with a heavenly meaning. This is the peace which we can see in its full glory only under the shadow of the cross to which we have brought our warring and restless hearts. This is the peace with God through the atonement of the cross, peace wrought through the sanctifying power of God the Holy Spirit, peace in a world that is without peace.

This is the only answer to the world's problems which can stand up in the light of eternity. Today it is time for more of us to see it clearly before it is too late. Much has happened in the world since the Unknown Soldier was laid to rest. But nothing has come over our days and our years which would shake the deep and consuming conviction that today as seldom before the world must wait, not for the man of the hour or the program of the moment, but for the God of the eternities and the plan of the ages. We have looked around for help. Now it is time to look up. We have tried to plan a new world. Now it is time to plan a new life. We have asked ourselves what we want. Now it is time to ask what God wants. Far more than pacts and treaties we need today the new promise of an old peace—the voice of the Eternal pouring itself into the agony of life without God—the last hope of a generation driven to its knees by the overwhelming realization that it has nowhere else to go: "Peace I leave with you; My peace I give to you; not as the world gives do I give to you."

There it is! The peace of the cross! Here is the profoundest need of our age. Often we may not be able to put it into words, but we know it in our hearts as we know nothing else. Some years ago Bertrand Russell summed it up in the following words: "Brief and powerless is man's life. On him and all his race the slow sure doom falls pitiless and dark. For him, condemned today to lose his dearest, tomorrow himself to pass through the gate of darkness, it remains only to cherish ere yet the blow falls the few hopes that ennoble his little life." I cannot see how men can live and die on that. There must be something which will make them glad and sure again, something to tell them that their brief mortal life has immortal meaning, something which will substitute for their deep dismay a peace and an understanding which the voices of despair and doubt can never give.

And the answer to this profound need lies in the simple words: "My peace I give to you." On these words rests the last unity of the human heart which it, unaided and alone, can never know. This is the true peace of the child of God in the kingdom of God. Peace — the peace which the world cannot give, the peace which comes from a surrendered happy faith in the atoning death of our Lord and Savior, the peace which passes the understanding of men, that comes and can come only from God. Long ago He gave it to the hearts of men through the obedient life and the atoning death of His only-begotten Son, Jesus Christ, our Lord. Through Him God spoke to the sin-stricken, hateful hearts of men finally and forever: "My peace I give to you." Yesterday, today, and tomorrow this was, is, and shall be the peace which men need more bitterly than anything else — the peace of forgiven sin — the peace of a heart redeemed by the blood of the eternal Son of God — the peace which rests forever and ever in the sure knowledge that without the fear of any law or command our hearts rest quiet and still in the God-given spirit-filled faith which comes from the Prince of Peace. We cannot remove hate and blood and fear from the world while our hearts are at war with God. We cannot stand united in anything but the most transitory and fleeting concerns of our brief interlude between the eternities unless and until we stand united in the blessed unity of heaven, the majestic company of the redeemed of God, bound together by a common hope, a common love, and a common faith in Him who even today holds in His cross-torn hands the last peace of the human heart.

And this peace of the cross is a very practical peace. While we may be concerned about the problems of the world—and God knows they are bad enough—we must be more immediately concerned about our own personal and individual problems. We cannot touch our world with the power of the conquering Christ unless we first look to ourselves, unless we view with deep concern any and all evidences which would rob us of the peace of the cross. Among ourselves we must watch daily for anything that might destroy our deep essential unity in the cross and leave us afraid and alone in this day of divine anger and winnowing. Our problem may be jealousy, envy, the love of material things, tiredness, restlessness—but whatever it may be, we must face it in the peace which comes from Christ and His cross. We must hear His voice again above all our human weaknesses and failures, above our personal problems, above all that may stand in the way of our becoming better and greater inhabitants of His blessed kingdom. "Peace I leave with you, My peace I give to you; not as the world gives do I give to you." Here is the last and ultimate hope of the human heart.

THE SIGN

of Understanding

And the Lord turned and looked at Peter. And Peter remembered the word of the Lord, how He had said to him, "Before the cock crows today, you will deny Me three times." And he went out and wept bitterly.

LUKE 22:61-62

I wonder if you have felt the air of seeming unreality which surrounds the words of our text: "And the Lord turned and looked at Peter. . . . And he went out and wept bitterly." This is one of the few silent moments in a night that was filled with shouting and lying and noise. One of the night's most significant events comes when two men suddenly look at each other. The hour was probably close to dawn. It was the end of a long and bitter night. Men were trying to get rid of their God.

Here there were now two men. One was only ten hours away from death. The other had just told a group of people around the fire that he did not know the Man who was going to His death. "No, no, I do not know Him. I have never been with Him. I swear I haven't."

And just then a cock crowed to greet the dawn. The Prisoner, apparently being led from one room of the palace to another, passed through the yard where the fire was. He looked at the man who stood there. Just a look! Suddenly the gate slammed, and out into the cold dawn fled the man who had been so loud and brave a moment earlier. He ran away and down the silent streets to hide himself in a corner of the great city; and as he ran, tears coursed down his face. They were hot and bitter tears, washing away something that was like dirt on his face and blood on his soul.

Certainly this is a strange scene. It is surely worth our time to examine it more closely. Just what happened there? I believe that the scene cannot be clear unless we understand that its meaning is far and deep and holy. Here at dawn, in one man looking at another, we catch a glimpse, revealing, terrifying, and healing, of the true meaning of the Christian faith.

Surely every thoughtful man or woman has at times asked the question: Just what is this religion which has held the world for almost two thousand years and to which most of us give some form of allegiance? There is a picture of it here in the courtyard at dawn. In the long history of Christianity some men have said that the Christian religion is essentially a system of doctrine to be believed. If you know the doctrines and believe them, you are a Christian. This is, of course, partially true; but this alone would not explain the look which our Lord gave Peter or the resulting sudden tears.

There are others who have said Christianity is really a way of life. Until recent years this has been the great modern heresy, particularly in our own country. This, of course, is also partially true. Christianity is in one sense a way of life. But this definition, too, is far from complete. No, this scene, as few others in the sacred record, shows again that Christianity is basically and essentially a living relation to a living Person. It is always and forever the relationship of a redeemed human soul to the redeeming

Person of Jesus Christ in faith, in love, in trust, in obedience, in all the ways in which one person is bound to another. This is really Christianity — nothing more and nothing less.

Now we can begin to understand what happened in the palace courtyard at dawn. As Peter was standing by the fire, lying for the sake of safety, swearing for a moment of warmth from the world's cold hate, he had broken that relationship to his Lord. He had thrown it away. He had turned against his Friend, his Savior, and his King. When his Savior turned and looked at Peter, he suddenly realized what he had done. He saw what he had thrown away and what he had forgotten. There was nothing to do but to stumble out into the dark, blinded by burning tears, afraid and alone, until another dawn a few weeks later when he would hear the voice of his Savior again, compelling, healing, and warm, by the lake: "Simon, son of John, do you love Me?"

It is now time for us to bring this story down to the twentieth century as quickly as possible. Certainly all of us, if we are honest with ourselves and with God, will have to say: "I have done the same sort of thing. Perhaps I have not done it quite so obviously or so publicly, but there have been hours when I have forgotten. I have broken the bond between Jesus Christ and my soul. I, too, have stood by the sputtering little fires of my lusts, my greed, my hate, my tongue, my envy, my malice. I have acted as if I had never heard of Jesus Christ."

It is perfectly clear that a pattern for denial of Christ was set that night. A denial always has four parts. (1) It begins with a bad situation. Peter should never have been standing by the fire. So also we, if we let ourselves in for situations which are made for a crack-up. (2) There comes the moment of forgetfulness. We want to be accepted by our environment. We want to be part of the crowd, no matter how bad and how evil it may be. (3) The break always comes. In our time and in our lives it is usually a denial by deed rather than by word. We do something which in its very nature is a denial of our Lord. (4) We can thank God that there is always the sign of understanding, the look of our Lord. Sometimes it is long in coming in the life of the individual. There may be years of seemingly getting by. But it is necessary that we mark it down: The look of our Lord always comes! He always turns around. Sometimes He looks at us in the still, small voice of our conscience, telling us that we did wrong. Sometimes He looks at nations in war and judgment. Sometimes He sees us in the voice of our pastor, the warning of a true friend, or a word from the Bible which suddenly strikes our mind and soul. He always turns around! He turns around to look at us and tell us that we are playing with life and with fire and dragging the sorrow of the ages across His soul, that we are breaking His heart and our own. If that realization leads to tears of regret and shame and repentance, then we, too, as Peter, are on the road to a new dawn, a voice tender, remembering, and forgiving: "My child, My child, lovest thou Me?"

It is vitally important for us to understand fully what His look can do. For this reason we ought to examine it very closely. What was there in the look of our Lord that brought Peter's world crashing about his ears and sent him out into the night in tears? Anger? No man who has merely been scolded has ever gone out into the night as Peter did. Reproach? Some, perhaps, but that was not all. The great, crushing power in that look, the elemental force which drove Peter into the night with heaven crying in his heart, the one thing that would remain with him in all the long and lonely years of wandering around the

Mediterranean world, the one great power which would lift him, keep him, and drive him, was understanding love. This, then, is the sign of understanding and of love. It was only a glance, but in that glance were all the golden memories of blessed companionship and all the infinite and gentle tenderness of the immortal Shepherd for one sheep that had lost the way home. "And [Peter] went out and wept bitterly!" In heaven the recording angel wrote his name, indelibly and forever, among those whom love had brought home again. This is the Christian Gospel. This is the sign of understanding and forgiveness. This is all of it. In it is the greatness of our faith and the power of it! This is the Gospel of another chance. This is the haunting, eternal voice of our Savior: "I have loved thee with an everlasting love."

There is an old tradition in the Christian church that this story has a very happy ending. It may be true, or it may be completely legendary, but it is singularly significant, with a certain justice and poetic fitness. It reports that on July 19 in the year of our Lord 64, thirty years after this night, a fire broke out in Rome. Half the city was destroyed. The Emperor Nero needed a scapegoat, and the Christians were at hand. According to the legend hundreds died by fire and the sword. Among them, according to the legend, was also Peter. At his own request he was crucified head downward because he did not consider himself worthy of dying in the same manner as his Lord had died. Here, then, the story ends. On a hot July morning an old man is hanging upside down in a Roman arena. If he opened his eyes, he saw the bloody red sand from which the church would grow in the years to come. But if he closed them, as I am sure he did – if he closed them in the moment of awareness and remembering of all the years that always comes to dying men – he saw something else. He saw many things in his own life, but surely above all, the dawn when he had looked into two eyes that understood him and loved him forever. He remembered the power that drove him out into the night to come at long last to this ridiculous position with the world upside down and tears of pain in his eyes once again. But now there was something else! He was waiting now for the moment when his Lord would come again to tell him that he had done well since that night, so well indeed that now the angels were waiting for him. He had kept the faith. And he knew, as he knew also that dawn by the lake, that now there would be no more night and no more tears. He was, I am sure, very content and very happy.

THE SIGN

of Agony

And being in an agony, He prayed more earnestly; and His sweat became like great drops of blood falling down upon the ground.

LUKE 22:44

All of us have learned how difficult it is to understand fully the sorrow and suffering of another person. To go beyond understanding to feeling is even more difficult. When tragedy strikes a friend, we can and should be sympathetic. We should suffer with him. However, we have also learned that no matter how hard we may try we can really never enter the inner recesses of the heart of another. This is where the last and deepest suffering takes place. Some time ago many newspapers reported the story of a little child who was run over by a truck driven by a friend of the boy's family. Anyone who read the story was deeply shocked. Hearts went out to the parents and to the neighbor who was so innocently the cause of the tragedy. Many expressed their sympathy. And yet the last measure of suffering and sorrow was beyond the reach of our words. We were not able to cross the final barrier between their lives and ours.

Of course, God could enter into this sorrow—right into the very heart of it—but not we. There are always inner recesses and corners of the human personality which another person cannot reach. It is inevitably and tragically true that the ultimate sorrow of the human heart and soul must be borne alone. I am certain you will understand why I mention this. The task we have set for ourselves in our Lenten worship tonight is even more difficult. We must try to understand as clearly as we possibly can the suffering of a Man, not in our own community but in a garden six thousand miles away in space and two thousand years away in time.

Furthermore, this suffering Man was not only man but also God. We must understand His suffering not only with our minds but with our hearts. We must really sympathize with—"suffer with"—at least a part of His sorrow. Some of His sorrow must become our sorrow, and some of His pain our pain.

Now one may legitimately ask the question: Why must we do this? There is only one answer. The suffering Man in the garden was and is our Savior. All of us were in His heart that night and that in a way which we can never fully understand on this side of the veil. We were a part of the agony of Gethsemane. The sin which we committed so easily and so carelessly yesterday or today was in that garden. It was the basic, ultimate, and terrible reason for the drops of blood, the sword in His heart, and the agony of His soul. The words of the great spiritual "Were You There When They Crucified My Lord?" also apply to Gethsemane. They come to us, even after all these years, with an insistent and powerful urgency. We were there.

There is, therefore, every reason for us to look very closely at the scene in the garden. Just what was going on there? What does it mean for our life and for our destiny?

Certainly it was a very strange situation. From time immemorial men had dreamed of God and the gods and of their meeting with divinity. They had built altars and temples for their deities. They had imagined the gods seated on Mount Olympus, or elsewhere, forever young, forever fair, aloof and cold. The gods were interested in men, but only to see to it that their laws were carried out and that transgressions of the laws of the universe were properly and inevitably punished. Gods were gods, and men were men. This was the way men thought the universe was arranged—before Bethlehem and Calvary.

Here now in Gethsemane, however, there is something amazingly different. Jesus Christ, God and man in one person, lies on His face beneath the olive trees. His sweat falls like drops of blood upon the earth. The immeasurable space around Him is filled with wheeling suns and stars which He has placed in the long whirling of the worlds. His hands—the same hands which were active at the creation of the universe—clutched the dust of the garden in agony. The Paschal moon—His moon—shines over waste oceans and waving treetops and looks down to light His face torn by an agony which was new on the earth.

Certainly there had never been anything like this in the long and bitter story of man. It may be that for some of us in this church now there will be in the years ahead some dark valleys, some agony of soul, some great loneliness. But we shall never know anything like this: all the world's aching sadness, this drying up of the fountains of life, this unimaginable sickening of soul. This was God and man suffering, and God can suffer more than men.

With this statement we are now beginning to touch the meaning of the scene, the reason for it, and the purpose of it. Perhaps there should be a warning at this point that many people will not want to see the true meaning of this agony under the Paschal moon. There may be various reasons for this reluctance to get close to it. Primarily, however, the reason lies in the fact that the true meaning of the agony in the garden is intimately, terribly, and eternally personal. It strikes every human being that has ever lived. It concerns every one of us in this church — and certainly we do not like to be directly involved in such terror of soul.

But there are also other human approaches to this agony. In order to soften the horror of the garden, men have said that His courage failed Him momentarily. He knew that in another twelve hours He would be dying on a cross. He was, they say, afraid of death. He did not want to go through with the next fifteen hours. This is obviously untrue. Could He have been afraid of death? Then He would have been weaker than many brave men who faced death without flinching. He would have been weaker than Stephen, whose face shone as the stones struck him. He would have been weaker than all the great company of martyrs, who met death gladly for His sake. He would have been even weaker than some of the men in this church tonight who looked squarely at death on the land, on the sea, and in the air during the days of war fifteen years ago.

No, it was nothing like that. He was not afraid of death or dying. If we look closely at His prayer in the garden, we see that He speaks to His Father not about tomorrow or what would happen on Friday afternoon. He is in agony over something that is happening right now. "This hour" — "this cup!" He is asking His Father in heaven to help Him in the climax of the atoning life and work which would go on until Friday afternoon. His agony of body and mind and soul was over something that struck Him under the olive trees with the disciples sleeping, the world at silent midnight, and the uncalled legions of angels looking on in horrified wonder. What was the real cause of His agony?

Anyone who is called to preach during Lent in this year of our Lord must say it very simply and clearly, again and again. It is the old, old story of sin and grace. What struck Him in the garden, pierced His soul, and painted incredible agony on His face was *sin*. There were voices, far and unheard, in the garden that night: "For our sake He [God] made Him to be sin who knew no sin." "The Lord has laid on Him the iniquity of us all." "Behold, the Lamb of God, who takes away the sin of the world." In some mysterious way known only to God, all the timeless sin and sorrow of all life and history gathered in His soul that night in the garden. All of it was there. None of it was missing. He bore it all, and He bore it alone. No one was with Him in the winepress of divine judgment.

Now we must again make this very personal and very up to date. That bit of gossip in which we indulged a few days ago; that lingering impurity in our lives; that murder in the newspapers of our great cities; the hate in our hearts; these massacres in the concentration camps and prisons of our world—all of these, all of these were on His head that night. He was sin! He was sin and evil incarnate during that hour.

And having said that, we still shall never really know what it fully means, because it was one of the great unique experiences of the God-man. It is the heart of our entire Christian faith—the total transfer of sin to the bleeding head in the garden and on the cross.

There is, however, one way in which we can understand it. We may never fully grasp its meaning for *Him,* but its meaning for us is perfectly clear. We can leave this church today quiet, free, and forgiven by faith in His atoning suffering as our Substitute. Our faces can now be calm and peaceful because His face was torn by agony. We can look up to God because He looked down into the lowest corners of hell. Every evil thing that worries us, every hidden sin, every fault we can leave in the garden with Him. He took care of it. It is His and no longer ours. This, you will understand, is the Christian religion – the religion of atonement, of redemption and forgiveness. And there is nothing else like it under the sun!

Perhaps there is one more thing that we should take from this service today. We should carry with us, too, the high and firm resolve to do a little better in the future than we have in the past. Pascal once said: "Jesus Christ is in agony until the end of the world." Upton Sinclair once wrote that one of the greatest causes of Jesus' suffering in the garden was the vision of what some of His faithless children would do to Him in all the years to come. And so today His agony is heard in all the sins of our time, in our carelessness with God and the suffering of all the images of God throughout the world. There is no greater way to live than to hear in all the pain and agony and horror of our time the echo of His agony, to resolve to help wherever we can, and to hear above the roar and confusion of our mad world His voice again and again: "Fear not, My child, I have already traveled that road. On each step of the terrible way I have left for you a drop of My blood and the print of My eternal mercy. Come in repentance and faith to Me, My lost and lonely child, and the way will always be clear and straight and bright for you." There is nothing greater and nothing more that you can possibly ask of God and His Son Jesus Christ, our suffering Lord. The cross is now, and always, the sign of His agony for us and the sign of our joy in Him and our salvation.

THE SIGN

of Decision

Now the chief priests and the elders persuaded the people to ask for Barabbas and destroy Jesus. The governor again said to them, "Which of the two do you want me to release for you?" And they said, "Barabbas." Pilate said to them, "Then what shall I do with Jesus who is called Christ?" They all said, "Let Him be crucified."

MATT. 27:20-22

As we go through life we find that there are many difficult lessons which we must learn. There are the lessons of sorrow, of pain, of joy, of discipline, of patience, of waiting on God to work out His purposes in our lives. Perhaps no lesson, however, is more difficult than the slowly growing awareness of the fact that God does not always work at the same speed. Sometimes for years in our own life and for centuries in the lives of nations nothing much happens. Life is smooth, quiet, and uneventful. Time is a slow river moving imperceptibly to the sea. There is a deceptive stillness about life and time which can easily lull us into a false sense of security. And then suddenly things begin to move, the clocks of the world and of life strike together, the river of time roars with confusion, and the chariots of the living God sweep through life and the universe. The God of life and history and redemption swings into visible and evident action.

This is exactly what happened on that first Good — and evil — Friday almost two thousand years ago. Many years ago an instructor in English asked his class: "What is the greatest single dramatic scene in all the world's literature?" The members of the class immediately offered some suggestions. Some mentioned the opening scene of *Hamlet* at midnight on the platform at Elsinore. Others referred to the death of King Lear in the storm, the murder of Duncan in *Macbeth,* or the knocking on the door in the stricken silence after the murder. The slamming of the door by Nora in the final scene of Ibsen's *Doll House* was mentioned. In Holy Writ itself the scene in the eighth chapter of the Gospel according to St. John between our Lord and the woman taken in adultery was cited. Finally the instructor said: "The greatest dramatic scenes in the entire world's literature are those which took place between six and nine o'clock on Good Friday morning."

This is probably true. Everything thinkable and unthinkable was going on. Every human passion was there: hate, anger, fear, love, pride, devotion. All the material of high drama was there: two trials, one murder, one suicide. There was always the tense waiting for the end.

It is a very curious drama too. It is held together only by the silent, mysterious figure of the leading Character, who speaks no more than one hundred words but who dominates the story as though He had rehearsed it from eternity. Here was God really moving fast, and when He moves, life and history and men move with Him to new, strange, but divinely appointed ends. He never moves alone.

Now we would like to present for your meditation

the great final turning point in this drama. We have now reached the point of no return. It is the moment when it becomes finally clear that the drama can end in only one way. This is the final slamming of the door! It is the moment which takes us out of our seats as spectators and makes us participants in the drama. We are in it now for all time and all eternity.

Let us look more closely at the scene before us. From the very beginning of the drama the heart of the action lies in the decision made by those who come face to face with the silent figure of the thorn-crowned Sufferer, our Lord and Savior Jesus Christ. To their dismay they find that they cannot remain neutral. They must make up their minds about Him. The hour of decision has come. And so one by one, with a weird consistency, they make up their minds about what they are going to do with their God on a quiet morning in spring. Judas decides — and commits suicide. Peter decides — and stumbles off the stage with blinding tears in his eyes. Annas and Caiaphas decide — and get a few more years of shoddy, uneasy power. The disciples decide — and flee into a night without stars. The stage empties faster and faster until now, at the moment which we are considering, this moment of turning, there are only four characters left — a Roman, a criminal, a faceless mob, and the silent, strange, leading figure of Jesus Christ.

Curiously enough, the one man who has the hardest time making up his mind about Christ is not one of the disciples but Pontius Pilate, the proud representative of a proud civilization. There are things inside him which seem to hold him back. He has a sense of fairness, of Roman justice, of patrician contempt for these quarreling people. On the other hand, he is a twentieth-century man. He has power, and he means to keep it. And so he twists and turns. He talks and temporizes in the vain hope that he may find some way to get off the hook, to avoid a decision, to discover some way out of the dilemma. He would like to find some way of getting rid of his God standing there in the morning sunlight, the living embodiment of another world.

Finally in his desperation he hits upon a seemingly brilliant idea. He does not want to decide, so, even as you and I, he will try to let someone else do it. Let the people decide! He resolves to be democratic about the situation and give them the choice between good and evil, between God and man, between Jesus and Barabbas. He appeals to the group morality involved in the problem. Surely they will decide the right way! Has not someone said that the voice of the people is the voice of God? Are not many minds better than one? Is there not something good, something fundamentally sound in the common man which inevitably and invariably rises to the challenge of goodness? We can almost see his mind at work. Surely the people will recognize the thorn-crowned Sufferer as one of their own, their Friend, their Teacher, the carpenter's son from Nazareth. Surely they will prefer Him to a murderer, a wild-eyed revolutionary, one of the anonymous criminals who were forever cluttering up the Roman jails all over the world. Surely this was an easy choice for the people! It was all so very clear and so very simple!

Today we all know what happened. Pilate asked his question — there was a roar from the crowd — and the noise of it was like the crack of doom in Pilate's ear: "Barabbas! Give us Barabbas!" The people had spoken. The election was over. The votes were in. The votes were counted, in earth and heaven and hell, finally and forever.

With this moment the scene becomes fearfully modern

and contemporary. We may call this what we please—spiritual blindness, mob spirit, moral insanity. We may refer to our texts on psychology and sociology in order to explain just what happened here. We must never forget, however, that this was a cross section of our common humanity. These were people even as you and I. They were men and women from the homes, the shops, and the markets of Jerusalem. Here were students from the school of Gamaliel, good people, religious people—people who would not think of killing an animal on Saturday, but who are ready to kill their God on Friday. We are reminded of the end of a great Spanish novel, *Blood and Sand,* in which the matador is dying and finally says, "I hear the roar of the only beast there is—humanity."

All this makes this scene very personal in its meaning for every one of us. Each of us in his own way must be a student of human nature. This is vital for a happy life. We must learn to get along with others. We want to know why people act as they do. Here—right here and now—is one of the great laboratories for such a study. Just why did the mob yell: "Barabbas! Give us Barabbas!"? Surely it was not because they hated our Lord Christ personally. Their leaders may have hated Him, but not the people themselves. He had come, as He had told them, to bring the Gospel to the poor, to bind up the brokenhearted, to tell captive souls that they were free, to open the eyes of the blind, to heal those that had been hurt and broken by life. My soul, you cannot hate anyone for that! No, we must understand clearly that there was something hopeless here, something deep and dark and demonic, something which you and I must face honestly if we are ever to understand human nature, life, and history. Here was something awful to see but necessary to understand. The people made their decision and cried "Barabbas," the world today cries "Barabbas," we cry "Barabbas," because they, the world, and we are under the deep, dark, demonic compulsion of sin. Here it is. All of it! It is clear and sharp in the morning sun. What was behind that cry on Friday morning is still behind it today. Sin! Cruelty, blasphemy, blind hate! All the whole vile catalog down to the last dregs of the lowest degeneracy. Every wrong appetite, every evil desire, every unnamed vice to the very last and the lowest of them all. Every sin of the world and in the world was there that morning. The sin of the past and the future, today's sin and yesterday's sin—this was behind the choice of the people. What was in the air that spring morning and is in the air in our own world is dark and evil. And so they cried "Barabbas!" James Russell Lowell tells of a painting in Brussels in which God is about to create the world and an angel is holding His arm: "If about to create such a world, stay Thy hand!" No, that is not the answer. It would be easy if we could blame all this on God, but God did not create a world of sin. This is our own doing. We can never blame anyone else for that.

Now, up to this point it is probably true that almost every realistic observer of the modern world would agree with what has been said. There seems to be no other way to explain what has happened to us, the way we dance and laugh on the edge of destruction, the seeming helplessness of the church, the dark, blind selfishness of men and nations. How can we explain this? All realistic observers will agree that it must be something like sin. There must be something really wrong with the very heart and soul of man. There must be something evil at the very core of human life, something which compels man to choose evil instead of God, which drives him to choose Barabbas again and again. In our time he usually chooses his own private, proud Barabbas, whoever or whatever he may be, just so long as he is a substitute for the living, redeeming God.

Concerning this many of us will agree. Now for the remainder of the truth which we confront today there will not be such universal agreement, perhaps not even in this church. It is now necessary for the preacher to present God's side of the story, a view that we can accept only by faith. It is at one and the same time simple and mysterious. If we in realism and penitence must identify ourselves with the people, God in His pity and grace identifies us with Barabbas, for whom our Lord became the Substitute, who went free because God was captive on a cross, who lived because Christ died. Now we are almost at the end of the story. This is what the theologian calls the mystery and miracle of grace. It always begins with a conversation between God and man. The conversation goes something like this:

Man, beaten and crushed: "I am a man of unclean life."

God: "I have redeemed you, you are Mine."

Man: "God, be merciful to me, a sinner."

God: "Rise, stand upon your feet, and I will speak to you."

Here, then, the final, great eternal miracle happens again. Man stands up free and forgiven because one day there was a cross and his sin entered into the life and heart of the eternal Son of God made man. It was shared by God. It was buried in God. And because this great decision was made by God, we can leave this church today heads up, free and forgiven. We will go out again into a world engaged in a gigantic, terrifying conspiracy of defeat. In his *Farewell to Arms* Ernest Hemingway makes the modern temper articulate: "The world breaks everyone, and afterward many are strong at the broken places. But those that will not break it kills either swiftly or by slow torture. It kills the very gentle and the very brave impartially. If you are none of these, you can be sure it will kill you, too, but there will be no special hurry." This is the approach of many modern minds to life itself. This is the hopelessness and helplessness of many of our contemporaries. We know that we cannot possibly live on this. We can live only when we know that God has mended the broken places and that we are strong and free where He has come. We are free and forgiven by the great decision which He has made by the might and measure of the glory of the cross.

Years ago a crowd was standing in a great square in London listening to the bell toll for the dead on Armistice Day. A man was standing in the crowd with his head bowed in prayer. A stranger spoke to him: "Do you really believe that these men are alive, that they are with God?" The man answered, "Yes." The stranger replied, "Yours must be a wonderful religion!" It is! It really is! When we know this, we are strong and safe in the full forgiveness of God for time and for eternity. God has made His decision, and by His grace we have made ours. And we have really made the right choice!

THE SIGN

of Mystery

*And when they came to the place which is called
The Skull [Calvary], there they crucified Him and the
criminals, one on the right and one on the left.*

LUKE 23:33

It was nine o'clock on Good Friday morning. It was
probably a fair and warm spring morning when the procession finally reached Calvary. Perhaps a little rain had
fallen during the night, as it does so often in the Holy
Land at that season of the year. The doves were circling
above the hill. The birds sang in the olive trees beneath
the city wall. It was a beautiful morning, a day for joy
and hope. It was an unusually good Friday.

I am certain that our Lord saw all that. He who
had watched the lilies of the field, the corn ripening for
harvest, the moon standing above the valley of the
Kidron — He would surely see once more the world as
God had made it, beautiful and fair, a world of song and
joy and hope, a world so far removed from the pain and
tears and blood and hate with which the procession came
to the little green hill beyond the gates of the Holy City.

And they crucified Him there! He was surrounded
once more by the strange continuing goodness of all His
creation except its crown, the body and soul of man, to

99

which evil had come. The rest of creation was so beautiful and fair, but the heart of man was black with evil and sin.

They began to dig the hole for the cross. The cross-pieces were fitted. His young body was laid on the beams. One nail was hammered home, then the second and the third. His arms and feet were bound tight with ropes because the nails might not hold the body racked with pain. Soldiers raised the cross upright. There was a dull thud as it fell into the hole dug for it. His blood started to flow from hands and feet. The aching, tearing pain of crucifixion began. They crucified Him there!

If we are really to see the meaning of the cross, we must now go to Calvary and stand there with Him. This will be very good for us. We must stand there, not as contemporaries, because it would be too easy for us to join the mob; we must stand there today as twentieth-century men and women, the seventieth generation since that first Good Friday. We stand there as the end products of 1,900 years of Christianity. We must stand at the edge of the crowd for a few moments and look very closely at the scene before us. Such an experience ought to be very much worthwhile, perhaps eternally decisive and ever-lastingly worthwhile.

Ever since Calvary there have been thousands of people in the world who have tried to make Christianity reasonable. Countless books have been written on the evidences of Christianity. They have been designed to prove that, after all, Christianity is a very reasonable thing, that you can think it through, that it appeals to the processes of thought and logic, the canons of human knowledge. Perhaps we should say again that much of this is very dangerous nonsense. The Christian religion is not a reasonable religion in the normal sense of the word. It is true, of course, that we can move around inside it by intellectual processes. We can formulate doctrines which are an exact reflection of the teachings of Holy Writ. We can reason from one proposition to another as theologians have done. We can work out conclusions on the basis of the inspired Word of God.

It must be said, however, that the great basic truths are always and forever beyond reason. We cannot prove them by the ordinary laws of thought. As we examine our Christian faith, we go farther and farther until ultimately we always come to a jumping-off place. We arrive at the place where reason ends. We come to the place where we stand either with folded hands or with hands holding a hammer. We stand in the place from which we must leap into the arms of God if we want to be Christians. Calvary is always a place of mystery and of wonder. It is the final, burning focal point of the strange heavenly ways of God with men. This we must always remember as we come to the cross ourselves, or when we try to bring others into its healing shadow.

Here, where we are now standing on the edge of the crowd at Calvary, is the ultimate mystery—the mystery of the cross. This is the riddle of God which can be solved only by God and in God and through His holy Word. We should freely admit that this just does not make sense in the way in which human beings interpret it. It is not reasonable—this cross, this mob, and God hanging there in the cool of a spring morning! As we stand there, the first question that comes to us is: What is behind all this? How did it happen?

The answer comes from faith, not from reason. We are face to face, as nowhere else in time and history, with the mystery of the evil in man. The last, dark, bitter mystery of sin! Many centuries ago St. Anselm said to a young man who had his doubts and misgivings about the

Christian Gospel: "You have not yet considered the seriousness of sin." It is true, of course, that our modern minds do not like this very much. We feel that, by and large, we are fairly good people. Our friends are fairly good people. People of other races and nations may sometimes be bad, but not we ourselves. Or if we are unusually intelligent, we go beyond this to say that the notion of man's essential sinfulness is unhistorical and unscientific. We must throw off this burden on man which has filled him with such a sense of guilt. We must now be ready to go forward to a religion of humanity. We must trust in the essential goodness of mankind. We must believe in our power to remake our environment. We must try to lift ourselves by our bootstraps into a new and better world.

No man can stand at the foot of the cross and believe in these notions. Here we are face to face with the mystery of sin. This is not a crowd of unreasonable, thoughtless men. This is a mob of bad men, evil men, who have come to crucify their God. The young man hanging on the cross is 33 years old. He had committed no crime. For three years He had been engaged in a tremendous mission of healing and love. He had gone about doing good. And yet they were now killing Him! The last thing He sees of humanity before He dies is a mob of grinning faces. The last thing He hears is a curse. The last thing He knows is hate and pain. Now, all this does not square for one moment with our theories of progress, our shallow belief in the essential goodness of humanity, and our false and fatal optimism concerning the destiny of the human race without God.

And so we turn again and again to our Bibles. There we find the answer to the mystery. We begin to believe and to understand the deep, dark problems which come to a climax at the cross. We find something which fits into our world and makes it much more understandable. We discover that sin is always hate. It is hate of God and man. It is the breaking down of all friendship and all fellowship between heaven and earth. It is the separation of God from man and man from man. We discover now the reason for the cross. It is the end of our long separation, our loneliness, our wandering, and our transgression. We had a love once, and we threw it out the window of our broken lives. We had a home once, and we turned away from it in hate and sin. We had a Friend once, and we left Him to die on the cross. The cross is only the last and ultimate expression of the dark terror in our souls, the bitterness of our lives, and all the brutality and tyranny and injustice and greed which have piled up since Paradise Lost.

Having looked to the darkness of sin, we now turn back to the cross to see some light in our darkness. Things become clearer. We begin to understand this ultimate mystery. It may be that we cannot understand everything, but we are beginning to find an answer to the question: Why is that young man hanging there? By His grace we know that He is God. Since He is God, where are the legions of angels? What keeps Him on the wooden bed of pain? Three nails? Those slivers of metal forged by human hands cannot possibly pin down God. There must be something else which holds Him to His dying! We have seen from Holy Writ the mystery of man and the mystery of sin. We are now face to face with the mystery of God. Our Lord Jesus Christ, the Savior of the world, is there on the cross because He wants to be there. He had wanted to hang there from the foundation of the earth, and He still wants to. It is neither the nails nor the new ropes that hold Him to His dying. It is just love and nothing else! It is the perfect love of the perfect God and the perfect love of a perfect man. Here we are face to face with the friendship of God pouring itself down and away through the cross. This is the miracle and the mystery of forgiveness. It is the restoration of fellowship with God and with man. We lost a friend, and He came back to us. We lost a love, and He gave it back to us. We lost a home, and He brought it back to the dust where we must live.

The mystery now comes a little closer to our human understanding. It is still a mystery, as everything about God is, but we can see that it is and why it is. It is all strangely simple with the profound simplicity of God.

There are men who say that Christianity is a very complex thing. They report that they find it difficult to find their way through its message. We, however, can never forget that all of it is in two sentences and that all of it is terribly personal. There is, first, always the cry of the defeated soul: "God be merciful to me, a miserable sinner." Then there is always the answering cry of the young Man on the cross, our Lord and Savior, "Father, forgive them; for they know not what they do." This is the whole story. Christianity is always the story of people who have come back again. David crying in the night, Peter stumbling into the dark in tears, Paul on the road to Damascus! Always and forever they dash the tears from their eyes because now they see life and time and sin and death and hate and pain with the eyes of Him who looked at us from the cross, saw us as we were and are, and loved us nevertheless. "While we were yet sinners" God, through His only-begotten Son, gave us life and peace.

Now for a moment we ought to leave Calvary and bring all that we have learned down to our own time and life. There is one more mystery about the sign of the cross. If we look hard at the world and history, we see its strange continuing power. This power needs more emphasis in our day, especially among those who have felt that the Christian Gospel is helpless over against the evil might of man. Too often we followers of our Lord Jesus Christ believe the Gospel, but we do not believe it hard enough. We approach it somewhat apologetically, and we bring it to men and women in the same way. Our attitude is much the same as the attitude of the pagan who said to his god, "Between us, I suspect that you do not exist." Our religion must be like an alpenstock which is so firm and sure and strong that it cannot be broken. We must have a faith which can stand up and take it! This means that we must stand at Calvary again and again in order to see the tremendous power of the love and mercy which broke the dominion of sin and gave us life and freedom and forgiveness.

To see this clearly is our task and our destiny, especially as twentieth-century Christians. To the seeing eye of faith the cross today is no longer a mystery. It is the strong power which stands alone above the fallen of the earth. It is the power of Him in whose eyes the past and the future are the eternal now. It is the power of Him who knows us even after all these years — us who own Him as King and Lord and who walk with Him through tears and tribulation and trial and time to the ultimate destiny of grace which He has laid up in heaven for us. It is the continuing power of Him who will come at last, not to a cross but to a throne. If we become His children, we have in Him, and in Him alone, the kingdom and the power and the glory forever and ever.

THE SIGN

of Power

Jesus came and said to them, "All power is given to Me in heaven and in earth."

MATTHEW 28:18

At first glance this would appear to be a strange text for a Lenten sermon. These are words spoken by our Lord several weeks after the darkness of Maundy Thursday and Good Friday. And yet, just because of this, they are worthy of our thought and meditation even today. They are true, eternally true, because of Maundy Thursday. The events of that dark and lonely night clearly reflect the truth of the words of our text: "All power is given to Me in heaven and in earth." These words are evident in our Lord's farewell address, in which He unrolled the carpet of history. They are the undertone of His high-priestly prayer, in which He carried the church of all the tomorrows to His heavenly Father in petition and far vision. They are very real in the first direct contact with His enemies. They become clear in His majestic and powerful silence before those who were killing Him, in all the minutes and hours of that lonely, tragic, and victorious night. Here we see, now more surely than ever before, that the sign of the cross, even at its darkest moment, is the sign of power.

It is very easy for the seventieth generation of the

men and women after the cross to lose the vision of its continuing power and victory. We have seen the tremendous contradiction between the faith proclaimed by the church and the faith by which men and women actually live and die in the streets of a mocking world. We see the tremendous odds against which the church of God must fight: the crushing weight of a decaying world, the awful gap between the faith we profess and the faith we live. We know that the things for which we stand and the faith by which we live are today openly hated and despised and cursed just as they were when men and women screamed their hate and defiance of God under a cross nineteen hundred years ago.

There is therefore always the immediate and imminent danger that our personal lives and the life of the church will be dominated by a crippling spirit of doubt, anxiety, and fear. There are many who feel that there is only weariness in the years before us: the pitiful stirring of burnt-out ashes of fires, the deadly routine of tending altars which the world has forgotten. We live in a world without much hope for a better tomorrow.

Such a spirit of doubt and fear is not Christian. It certainly should not be part of our memory of Maundy Thursday and Good Friday. There is a continuing power about the cross which towers over the momentary wrecks of time. Everything else may change. The truths by which men attempt to live may sink into chaos and night, the world may grow weary and old, but in the cross of Jesus Christ is the fountain of eternal power and everlasting youth. This year of our Lord, like every other year, is still under the sign of the cross — the sign of power!

Although the church seems to be beaten back from one area of human life after another and apparently lives only on the crumbs of men's time and talents, it is nevertheless true that as long as she lives close to the cross, she is the most powerful phenomenon in the modern world. The Scriptures testify to the fact that the entire period of the New Testament church, which began with the sunrise of Calvary and will end only with the last red sunset of the world, is a day of power and victory. "All power is given to Me." As members of the church we stand in the long tradition of the day of power against the night of weakness which men have made for themselves. As we sing our hymns and speak our prayers on Maundy Thursday and all other days of the year, we are in line with all the true power of two thousand years. The sudden light over Bethlehem, the Man from Nazareth who spoke words as never yet man spake, the dark hour on Calvary and the glorious hour in the resurrection garden, the long years with their red line of saints and martyrs, the conquering faith of crusader and scholar and reformer — all these testify to the continuing power of the cross. They lived under the sign of power!

Today we may sometimes feel that the center of power has really finally shifted elsewhere. Surely men no longer live and die for God and Christ and His church. They live by guns and fear and hate. They follow hypnotic voices shouting to the ends of the earth. And yet again and again the continuing power of the cross demonstrates itself in the lives of men. It is strange how often modern man, pausing for a moment in the madness of life without God, sees the power of the Crucified on the dark horizon of his world. Somehow he seems to know that the figure of the Son of God bearing the sins of the world is the answer to all the problems which trouble and perplex the souls of men. He feels something which he has lost. It is this sense of power which the church in our time must again recover and proclaim to a dying world. We must again be stirred by our Savior's words: "All power is given to Me." We must be alive to the promise of the cross, that by its everlasting power it can make, through the forgiveness of sins, our succession of common days a triumphant march to a better world and the high fulfillment of our cross-given destiny. Seeming defeat will be turned into victory. Human indifference and human bitterness will only cause us to turn from earth to heaven, and our human weaknesses will compel us to turn to the cross for strength and hope and power.

The life of the world and the individual proceeds by twos. There is an evident duality in life: body and soul, good and evil, light and darkness, night and day. One day this duality will end. There will be only one victory — and it will be ours! Through the shadows of Maundy Thursday and Good Friday, through the darkness of the evening time of the world our eyes must be fixed once more today on the cross of Jesus Christ, eternally young, eternally strong, and finally eternally victorious. It is the great continuing sign of power!

And now the strange, mysterious thing about all this is that men must be driven to their knees before they can really see the ultimate meaning of Maundy Thursday and Good Friday. Driven to their knees by the consciousness of their sin, by the breaking down of fellowship with God, they are completely ruined. Sin is bad in the world, worse in the church, and worst of all in the relationship between God and man. Have you ever noticed how every reference in Holy Writ uses this picture? Sin is wandering, loneliness, going away, going astray, separation. There is always the same tolling theme! We have lost the power to make our life strong and full of hope.

On Maundy Thursday and Good Friday we see now the amazing, humanly incredible sign of the power of the cross. This is the power and miracle of forgiveness, the restoration of fellowship, the return to the Father's house. In our Lord and Savior's suffering on Calvary our brokenness is healed and our union with God and man restored. Our great separation, so long now and so bitter, has been ended by the reunion with God through Jesus Christ. The bonds of sin are loosed. We have again the freedom beneath and beyond all human freedoms: the freedom from fear of sin, the freedom from want of God, the freedom of worship of God, the freedom of speech to God! Maundy Thursday and Good Friday tell us that this is an accomplished fact. We are facing a finished redemption. In our time, too, many men have made an effort to make our faith a quest instead of an achievement! As Christians we must say to them that in contrast to all other religious systems the faith of Christianity is a fact, done and complete, and not a search for higher truth. The essence of Christianity is that something has been done and nothing remains to be done. It is finished—holy, powerful, and perfect!

And how that message fits into our world with its haunting sense of incompleteness, of unfinished faith, of broken dreams and lost hopes. This is our faith: "Only once in the long story of our incompleteness there was one task that was done completely, finally, and absolutely." It remains now as the last continuing sign of power over the world. Our Lord's atonement gives us the power to stand up before God, ladies and gentlemen of His choosing, unashamed and unafraid. This is the heart of our great faith. It is good for us to remember it once more this Maundy Thursday and to live by it—and perhaps to bring it to our world, however haltingly and humbly, so that others, too, might come under the sign of the power of the cross.

THE SIGN

of Finality

Jesus said, "It is finished!"

JOHN 19:30

"Father, into Thy hands I commend My spirit."

LUKE 23:46

Fifteen hundred years ago St. Anselm ascended his pulpit on Good Friday and said: "I do not know if I wish to speak today. Why should I speak when my Savior is silent and dies?" Certainly every preacher has felt much the same way. All he can really ask his people to do is think quietly and personally about the meaning of the cross, now that the great drama draws to its close.

Today, therefore, we wish to consider, in Good Friday humility and silence, two sentences at the very close of the scene on Calvary. They are probably the greatest in all the history of human speech. They cover all of life and the shadow of death. The first is "It is finished!" By this we can live. The second is "Father, into Thy hands I commend My spirit." By this we can die. To think about these two sentences is therefore a very good way to spend a part of Good Friday.

Let us look at the setting. It is now about three o'clock in the afternoon, the last few moments in the drama of the cross. The crowd has become a good deal more quiet.

Even mobs become still when death rides. Suddenly the head goes up once more under the crown of thorns, and in a loud voice our Lord and Savior says, "It is finished!" The meaning of this sentence must be perfectly clear to all of us. To the Pharisees standing around the cross, to the Roman soldiers, if they had eyes to see and ears to hear, these words must have sounded like the crack of doom. Had they after all lost? They were killing Him, but He seemed to feel that He had won a victory. Yes, if they had eyes to see and ears to hear, they would have seen each thorn in His crown become a shining gem in His diadem of glory. They would have seen the nails forged into the scepter of a king. They would have seen His wounds clothe Him with the purple of empire. He had won a great, final, and eternal victory. The world was changed. Until the end of time history would now be divided into before and after. He had won a victory which was decisive for all men. All men would now have to decide on their attitude over against the cross. There could be no neutrality. From this moment on He would be either a stone of stumbling or the Way of life and to life.

If we look more closely at our Lord's dying words, "It is finished," we see that He is not referring to the fact that His agony is now ended, that the malice, the hatred, the pain, the heart broken with sorrow are now done and set aside forever. Nor is He merely saluting death as so many brave men have done before and since Good Friday. Nor is He merely saying good-bye to life, the years flashing swiftly before His mind, tired of Himself, tired of life, as Hamlet said, "To sleep, perchance to dream" and "The rest is silence." No, it should be perfectly clear that this is the cry of a worker whose work was done, of a soldier whose warfare was ended, of a Savior whose work had been accomplished. We of the twentieth century must be especially sure of this. He has in His grip these days and these years and what we have done to Him and to one another. His is the power and the glory forever and ever.

For proof of this we can, of course, turn to the pages of Holy Writ to find echoes of His final cry. "Wherefore God also hath highly exalted Him and given Him a name which is above every name, that at the name of Jesus every knee should bow." There are many passages like this. Today, however, we should like to point to another proof which reflects the full meaning of His words, "It is finished." Let us turn for a moment to His enemies, to the indifferent, some of whom are in the churches of Christendom today. They are one of the great testimonies to His continuing power. They simply cannot leave Him alone! His enemies still hate Him. Men do not hate the dead. Hate dies when the object hated dies. No one today hates Napoleon or Genghis Khan. Men no longer clench their fists against a Bismarck or stand guard over the tomb of a Nelson. But they still clench their fists against Christ, and they still stand guard over His tomb. They say He is helpless and dead, but they pour out literature against Him and His church. They build philosophies of government and life constructed to shut Him out. They clench their fists when His very name is mentioned. Why? Men do not fight ghosts. There are two kinds of faith: the saving faith of the redeemed and the protesting faith of the damned, and both of them always testify to the sign of power in Christ and His cross. We see evidence of His continuing power in the books His enemies write against Him, in their laughter over His church, in their cynicism concerning the power of His Gospel. Day after day, as long as the world stands, His enemies testify to His mysterious hold over men and life and time.

Why? Francis Thompson in "The Hound of Heaven" writes a line which sums it all up. He points clearly to the reason why men still look at Jesus strangely as He passes by in life and in history. For time and eternity it is true, as Thompson says, "All things betray thee who betrayest Me." That's it! All things betray man when he betrays his Lord and Savior Jesus Christ. All the good things in life which He made, love and laughter and sunshine and health, become dust and myrrh and ashes without Him. On Good Friday more men and women know it than on any other day of the year. Perhaps that is the reason for the crowded churches. Once more they feel the strange, mysterious power of His words, "It is finished!"

We who by His grace and pity have made His victory our victory can now live on and on by His cry, "It is finished!" Our sins are now forgiven. Our souls are cleansed. Our consciences are clear and clean. Our incompleteness has ended in His final word. Our unfinished tasks and our broken lives are complete, finished, and made whole by Him who loved us so much that He would rather die than be without us. His cry, "It is finished," makes it clear that we now, too, can join in His victory.

Every thoughtful man and woman knows that the greatest continuing and haunting sorrow of life is just its sense of incompleteness, of unfinished tasks, of things that we would like to do and cannot do. Life is full of loose ends and frayed edges. Of course, we often say, "This is done and finished," but what we mean to say is, "It is the best I can do just now. Perhaps someday I shall be able to do better." So the end of anything in life is never complete and final. Time and life are much too fluid for that.

Here, however, on the cross we have in the long story of our incompleteness and imperfection one task that was done completely, finally, and absolutely by any standard

114

of measurement, human or divine. The work of our Lord from the first cry in the manger to the last cry on the cross was a divine symphony coming to its final and inevitable end. "It is finished!" And with the finishing of His task our sins are forgiven, and we stand before God in the complete perfection of His atoning life and work.

The second sentence is equally important. "Father, into Thy hands I commend My spirit." Here is something by which we can die. Men have always been interested in the way humanity has met death. Men's dying words are always significant. Macbeth said: "Out, out, brief candle; life's but a walking shadow." Goethe cried: "Light! More Light!" Anatole France said: "Draw the curtain; the farce is played out." Men have faced death in protest or in shrugging acceptance. They have run the entire gamut of emotions when they are face to face with the final and universal fact of life.

There is nothing like that in our Lord's last word. His head goes up once more. He is now facing His heavenly Father alone. The crowd has been forgotten. The pain of the crucifixion is almost in the past. He is coming home now, the long adventure over, carrying in His hands the atonement which He has made for all the sins of the world. In the great halls of heaven cherubim and seraphim wait for Him, the tall lilies of heaven bend left and right, and the choirs of eternity stand silent. He has commended His spirit into the hands of His heavenly Father. We know that all the angels rejoice because the one poor thief with Him is the first of a long procession of men and women who will storm the gates of heaven with His blood covering their sins and His love bringing them home. This is a great and goodly company. By faith in His atoning work we, too, can join them.

We have all seen a mother putting her child to bed.

The child protests. It wishes to stay up just a little longer. There are so many things still to be done. And so also we, when the final word comes to us. Toward twilight we hear a voice saying to us: "Now put away your toys, the little things with which you worked in life, the patchwork of your plans and your dreams. It is time for you to say your prayers and go to sleep." We, too, shall ask for just a little more time, a few more hours.

But then something great and wonderful and eternal will happen just as it happened to our Lord on Good Friday. We, too, will commend our spirit into the hands of our heavenly Father. And as for Him, so also for us, there will be another morning — the great morning of God. We shall wake up to see something very splendid and very beautiful. Flaming and glowing on the tapestries of heaven will be all the little things which we began to do and tried to do here on earth, cleansed, glorified, and transfigured by Him who has preceded us and who now pleads for us before the throne of His heavenly Father through all eternity. He has finished our little tasks for us. They have been finished by hands that once were torn by nails and that reached out for heaven at the last moment.

There is a great medieval picture of Calvary which tells this story better than mere words. At first glance it is the usual picture of the crowd and the three crosses. But over in the corner there is a man taking off his shoes! There is peace and joy in his face. He is taking off his shoes because here at Calvary he has come home. So in all the churches of Christendom today, all those that stand in the light of the cross have come home to the home of warmth and love and no loneliness at all. This is the power of the cross also over the final fact of death.

It remains for us, as another Good Friday comes and goes, to tie all the loose ends together so that they can never break. Down in the gutter of the city street there is a drop of water, stagnant, soiled, and dirty. From far up in the heavens the sun falls upon it, warms it, fills it through and through with its strange new life, lifts it up higher and higher, beyond the clouds. Then one day it falls as a snowflake, white and clean and pure, on a mountaintop. This is the whole story of our life in Christ and with Christ. Our own lives, often so soiled, so tawdry, so low, and so worn, can be lifted on the wings of the morning if we give them to Him who once was lifted up on Good Friday and who commended His spirit into the hands of His heavenly Father. We, too, can be lifted up until we walk the high places of the earth, unashamed and unafraid, living in the company of Him who died that we might have life and have it more abundantly, for His is the kingdom and the power and the glory forever and ever.

And so He goes home now to His Father on that first Good Friday; and, as we watch Him go, what shall we say? Perhaps only the old intimate words:

> Your arms are strong around me, and I know
> That somehow I shall follow where you go,
> To the still land beyond the evening star
> Where everlasting hills and valleys are.
> And evil shall not hurt me any more,
> And terror shall be past, and grief and war.

"Father, into Thy hands I commend My spirit." Certainly there is no better and no greater way to die than that. This is the ultimate, final sign of the finality of the cross.

THE SIGN

of His Presence

But they constrained Him, saying, "Stay with us, for it is toward evening and the day is now far spent." So He went in to stay with them. When He was at table with them, He took the bread and blessed, and broke it, and gave it to them. And their eyes were opened and they recognized Him, and He vanished out of their sight. They said to each other, Did not our hearts burn within us while He talked to us on the road, while He opened to us the Scriptures?

LUKE 24:29-32

Few stories in the entire Sacred Record are more dear to the Christian heart than the story of Emmaus. Here in a few sentences all the comfort and glory of Easter are applied directly to the problems of life and living. Here we see, clearly and finally, the meaning of the open tomb for our own journey toward the last sunset. The entire story is a striking parable of human life. It began in confusion and pain and ended in faith and joy. It began in darkness and ended in the white light of the Sun of Righteousness. It began in loneliness and ended in the magnificent truth that since Easter morning no believing heart need ever be alone again.

The story itself is familiar to Christian memory. On

the afternoon of the first Easter Day many years ago, two of the sorrowing disciples, weary with the black memory of Good Friday, were walking toward Emmaus. Their hearts were filled with sadness and fear. They were face to face with the end of everything they had hoped and believed. Three days had come and gone since the news of His death had reached them. Nothing more had happened. True, a few of the faithful women had been at the sepulcher that morning and had astonished them by reporting that the body was not in the grave. That, however, seemed to be only a wild rumor.

As they walked and talked, our Lord joined them on the way. Their eyes, dark with sorrow and blinded with tears, did not recognize Him. He asked the reason for their sadness. They told Him the story of the mighty words and deeds of Him whom they had now lost, of His shameful death, of the ruin of all their hopes and dreams, and of the strange report of the women on that third morning. Their recital ended with the simple, sorrowing report that they "did not find His body." No matter what they had heard, they wanted to see Him. If only they could see Him once more! If only they could know that He was alive! Then all that had gone before would be as a momentary dream in the night, lost and forgotten in the light of His presence.

And then the Stranger spoke! "And beginning with Moses and all the prophets, He interpreted to them in all the Scriptures the things concerning Himself." He reached far back into the dawn of time in order to show them why Good Friday and the cross had to come. He spoke of Moses and David and Isaiah. He showed them how the prophets had foretold everything that had happened. This was no sudden and unexpected event planned and executed by the powers of darkness. All of it, every single

119

step, was a part of the eternal counsels of the Holy Trinity, conceived in eternity and executed in time: "Ought not Christ to have suffered these things and to enter into His glory?" This was the great divine "ought," the eternal "must." All these things ought to be, He told them, in order that through the glory of Bethlehem, the pain of Good Friday, and the victory of Easter the souls of men might be redeemed.

But still they knew Him not! Only after He had gone in to tarry with them, the simple little act of breaking the bread and blessing it suddenly opened their eyes so that they knew Him. Perhaps their memory suddenly went back to the days when they had seen Him do this in Galilee and Judaea. "Their eyes were opened and they recognized Him." The grave was really empty! Their Lord was alive! He had won the final victory over death. Now they knew that Easter had come.

Many centuries before the still dawn of Easter Day a great cry, wrung from the heart of Job, began to echo across the waiting ages: "I know that my Redeemer lives." Taken up and repeated by countless saints, in the years of life and the hours of death, it became the great, eternal message of the open grave and the empty tomb. Early in the morning the women hurrying to the grave with the sorrow of death returned from the grave with the joy of life. The stunned silence of the disciples, torn between the warm faith of their hearts and the hard fact of the cross, became the everlasting antiphon for the voice of Job. "I know that my Redeemer lives." All the ages could now sing it, and all men could now know it. The stone rolled away had been made by the hand of God a witness to His eternal power and a monument to His living presence.

The story of Emmaus has been repeated countless

times since that first Easter evening. By the grace of God it can also be our story. Its courage and victory can come also to us, who live so far down the ways of time. "Stay with us, for it is toward evening and the day is now far spent."

One of the dark marks of our time is its uncertainty. Men are not sure of anything. In fact, it has become fashionable to doubt. It is considered smart and sophisticated to be uncertain. The result has been ruin and death. In such an age nothing is more desperately important than the question: Is there anything that is sure and permanent in life?

The answer lies in our Easter faith. There is nothing vague or mysterious or indefinite about it. Its message is that Christ lives. He lives with us. He lives for us. A believing child can understand this. It is clear and sure. It is a fact witnessed by history and certified by faith.

Just how does He live with us? Although He ascended into heaven on the afternoon of Ascension Day, He did not leave the disciples afraid and alone. Within a few days they became a conquering host. Confounded and appalled by the tragedy of Good Friday, huddled behind locked doors in hidden houses in Jerusalem, they became the indomitable bearers of the cross, the men and women before whom the Roman Empire began to tremble. If they became living faggots, they knew they were torches of the Gospel. If they died, their faces at the moment of death were like Stephen's, the "face of an angel." They lived "under the long looks of God and His glances of a thousand years." Why? Because He had answered their prayer "Abide with us" with the great sentence which ends all loneliness and fear for the Christian heart: "Lo, I am with you always, to the close of the age." It is true that we cannot see Him with our eyes or touch Him with our hands. He has His own way of being with us in the world. It is a great and a sure way. It stretches beyond and above the noise of the world and the dark highways of men as the great, shining highway of the King of kings. This way lies in His Word and His sacraments. He comes to us through these means of grace. In them and through them He enters our hearts. There is no other way by which we can live in His abiding presence. No good works or seemingly holy life will bring Him to us. At Emmaus the disciples remembered that He had opened the Holy Scriptures to them: "Did not our hearts burn within us while He talked to us on the road, while He opened to us the Scriptures?" So He comes to us today through His Word, and our eyes are opened to His presence by His grace. When He ascended from the earth in His glorified body to rule the centuries from the right hand of His Father in heaven, He left us His life, His death, His forgiveness in the pages of the Holy Scriptures and in the sacraments. Through them the story of Emmaus was to be repeated again and again, every day and every hour of Christian history. By them the Comforter was to bring faith into our sorrowing hearts and companionship to our lonely lives. They were to bring us the blessed assurance of the forgiveness of sins, peace, and salvation.

Do not our hearts burn within us as we remember today how often we have neglected these means of His coming into our lives? On the way to Emmaus the eyes of the disciples were darkened by sorrow and fear. Somehow they had to be opened again to the glory and power of His abiding presence. Today, when our hearts are so often shadowed by the darkness of hate and blood, by our countless fears over the future, by the storms of war, dare we neglect the only way in the world by which faith and courage and hope can come alive again in our eyes?

This is the way to Emmaus—with Him. Even today it winds past the noise and confusion of the world to the pulpit and altar of our church and to the Bible in our homes. There our Lord waits to answer all our questions and end all our fears.

By the grace of God this can be our first lesson today: Our risen Savior abides with us in His Word and sacraments. When we use them faithfully, regularly, frequently, He draws near to us. Our eyes are opened and we see Him. Our faith beholds Him as He was foretold by prophets, born in the manger, dying on the cross, breaking the tomb, so that He may now abide with us forever, here by the means of grace and there by the vision of glory. This is most certainly true!

Everything our Lord does is done for us. We are the objects of His eternal love. When He comes to us and abides with us, He has certain definite purposes in His mind and heart. He wishes to give us something. His presence means something great and beautiful. The disciples at Emmaus knew that. Their plea "stay with us" was based on the statement "for it is toward evening and the day is now far spent." It was growing dark. The Stranger who had opened the Scriptures to them would be good company for the coming night. As they had listened to Him, their hearts had burned with a new courage and a far hope. They wanted Him to stay with them because in His presence they had found a new understanding of the counsels of God and their meaning for history and life.

This has always been the blessed experience of the believing heart. The presence of the risen Savior changes everything in life. Absolutely everything! Forty days after Emmaus He was standing with His disciples on a hillside in Galilee. His voice came to them like the rush of mighty waters which would tear them from their moorings and hurl them over the Roman Empire. "Go therefore and make disciples of all nations." Because of the magnitude of this task He immediately added the words which repeat the shining story of Emmaus: "Lo, I am with you always, to the close of the age." Although a cloud was about to take Him away from their sight, no cloud and no shadow would ever come between Him and the vision of their faith. If happiness was to come to them, it would be the happiness reflected from the light of His presence; if honor, it was to be the honor of Calvary; if glory, it was to be the glory of His love. He would abide with them forever.

This must be our prayer after these many years. If we ask Him, He always stays.

Countless men and women have lived and died in His presence for almost two thousand years. It is still the best way to live and to die. The entire Holy Scriptures end with the moving words, "Come, Lord Jesus." Whenever and wherever these words are spoken in repentant faith, we hear His answering voice, old and lovely, healing and tender, "Yea, I come quickly." He crosses the threshold of our hearts, and life can never be the same again. In the continuing mercy of His presence we can forget the huge invisible load of care and sin, the intolerable burden of the remembered years, and all the cares and sorrows which make life so dark for the men and women who walk the ways of the world without Him.

This is what His abiding presence can do for us also today. As seldom before in the history of the world, men have lost their faith in manmade things. They have found that education and science cannot give the final answer to the problems which trouble and perplex the souls of men. They are haunted by a feeling of failure and defeat.

Also the Christian heart is sometimes touched by this universal feeling of futility and despair. When we look at our own lives, we find that we are seldom completely happy. We are aware of our own weaknesses and defeats. We remember old sins and old troubles. We feel that the world about us is rushing toward destruction. Our weary hearts cry out for the living God, for the calm peace and sure rest which can be found in Him alone. The Easter message of the abiding presence of the risen Savior is the only possible solace and comfort for our ills. It tells us that we can now live with Him who took all our troubles and sins up to Calvary and buried them in the forgiveness of God. It assures us that through the forgiveness of sins we can begin each day anew. As we walk with His nail-torn hands in ours, life begins to move and live. It is no longer a dull routine. We live with Him. He knew its meaning and purpose. The world may say: "Happy is the man who is rich, who is powerful, who is popular, who enjoys life, who can do what he wants to do." Our Savior tells us that the world is fearfully wrong. Across the tears and the graves of those who thought that the world was right He comes into our lives to tell us that with Him there is a new set of standards and an eternal value and importance in our brief journey between the cradle and the grave. In His presence we cannot be afraid, because He is not afraid; we cannot be dismayed, because He is not dismayed; we cannot be conquered, because He will not be conquered. Facing all the storms and tears of life, there is always Someone by our side who knew them all and suffered them all for our sakes.

This is the continuing power and glory of our Easter faith. As the shadows of time lengthen and the hour of man grows late, we shall need this faith more than ever before. Much work remains to be done in the world so that the message of the risen Savior may be brought to new millions sitting in an old darkness. Finally, only the men and women who live in the abiding presence of the King of kings can bring peace and hope to the hurt and bewildered souls of men.

Our Savior's company can never be an excuse for idling and drifting through life. While He gives us peace for our souls, He also gives us work for our hands. Since we live with Him, we have the blessed privilege of bringing Him to others who do not know the grace and power of His presence. Our days and years belong to Him, and He asks us to use them for Him until the night comes. Just as the disciples at Emmaus hurried back to tell others that they had seen their Lord, so we are called to go out into the world of our friends, our neighbors, and our enemies and tell them of His everlasting grace and mercy.

"Stay with us, for it is toward evening and the day is now far spent." Let this be our humble and heartfelt prayer as we again behold the glory of Easter and its meaning for us. Let it be for us the assurance that in the Word and sacraments our Savior is here with us and will never leave us nor forsake us. Let it be for us a challenge to work for Him and with Him while we wait for the day when He will come again to translate our faith in His abiding presence into the vision of His eternal victory.